FROM
HOLLYWOOD
TO
WREXHAM

FROM
HOLLYWOOD
TO
WREXHAM

PETER READ

First impression: 2023

The publishers wish to acknowledge
the support of the Books Council of Wales.

Cover design: Y Lolfa

ISBN: 978 1 912631 45 2

Published and printed in Wales
on paper from well-maintained forests by
Y Lolfa Cyf., Talybont, Ceredigion SY24 5HE
website www.ylolfa.com
e-mail ylolfa@ylolfa.com
tel 01970 832 304

CONTENTS

CHAPTER I

TELLING THE STORY

THIS IS THE story of two mega Hollywood stars taking over a football club in the Vanarama National League. In other words, a club in the fifth tier of English football. A division where some sides attract crowds of only 800 on a regular basis. But before we get to meet the two incredibly important main characters, it's also my story. After all, they took over my club.

It's important to know how and why, being born just inside the Welsh border, I chose to follow Wrexham Football Club. I suffer from a disease called Wrexhamitis. Massively successful clubs, such as Everton, Liverpool, Manchester United and Manchester City, are less than an hour from my birthplace in Rhosllanerchrugog, and in the other direction Aston Villa or West Bromwich Albion are also pretty close. Yet, I still contracted Wrexhamitis when I was 11 years old. It descends on me most Saturday afternoons and some Tuesday nights. There is no drug to wipe it out and, as far as I know, no rehabilitation centre with a programme to cure footballholics. The illness makes me either manically depressed for long periods, or manically happy for shorter periods of time. So, before we summon Hollywood into the story, it's important I tell you about the early signs that I was destined to be a Wrexham fan for ever, following the team that played at the Racecourse Ground, just four miles from my birthplace.

HOOKED

When I was seven years old, I scored 32 goals in one game. It's pointless checking the record books. You won't find any reference to my amazing feat. It was a one-on-one match against my friend Paul. It took place in his garden. His goal was one garden wall and mine was the other. I shimmied my way past him with a cross between a dummy and a bulldozer. When I got to his goal (otherwise known as the wall) which was now unguarded, I easily slotted the ball (as reporters would say) into the empty net (bricks in the wall). I scored one goal, then another, and another right up to 32. I had no idea I was supposed to bring the ball back to the centre circle after a goal had been scored. While all this was happening, Paul had given up the ghost, not literally, but figuratively. Bored, he didn't even bother to try and retrieve the ball from me. He just lay on the ground, looking up at the sky, ignoring my escalating joy at the other end of the garden. So the score stood as a never-to-be-repeated 32–0 to me.

A SMALL BOOK BRINGS GREAT CHANCES

When I was ten my father bought me a football annual published by the Stoke *Sentinel* newspaper. The book contained fixtures for the forthcoming season of all four divisions of the English Football League. It also carried the final tables for the previous season of all amateur leagues in Staffordshire. I was clueless about how to work out league tables. As all football fans, and as I now know, P W D L F A P stand for Played, Won, Drawn, Lost, For, Against, Points. My ten-year-old brain told me that you tot-up all the figures. This caused mayhem and confusion. A useless team who'd lost most of their games and conceded over 100 goals should, by my reckoning, be top. Mercifully my father put me right. I'm so glad he intervened. Otherwise I could have spent my life as the most embarrassing football fan ever to enter a pub.

Suddenly I was a footballholic. I hungered for facts, read newspaper reports and learned information about each professional club in my annual. The name of every ground was remembered. Nicknames fuelled my childish imagination. My own headlines were: Toffees smash the Hammers (Everton v West Ham United); Hatters clip Bluebirds (Luton v Cardiff); Tigers swallow Foxes (Hull City v Leicester City); Robins shoot Gunners (Wrexham v Arsenal). I very quickly knew not only the names of all the grounds but also the clubs' managers. When I felt I'd memorised what I wanted to know, I sunk to the lowest of the low. I began learning the phone numbers of the grounds. It's true. Not all of them, just some of them.

As an adult, if unable to sleep, I don't count sheep. I count football club telephone numbers. Working through the alphabet I know that when I get to 01904 624447 it's time to get up and make a drink. York City. Forget football. Welcome insomnia with PG Tips. You can't go any further, so don't even try, say the powers-that-be at York City.

HOW WILL I SEE
MY FIRST PROFESSIONAL MATCH?

Jealous of boys in primary school who were taken to see professional football by their parents, I had to do with creating my own virtual world of football action. As a devoted member of the Plymouth Brethren Christian Church, my father believed it was wrong to mix with unbelievers. This meant there was little or no chance of me ending up at the Racecourse to watch Wrexham. I could have argued that all those going to the ground every game must be believers. After all, they cheered for a team stuck in the Fourth Division. Somehow I don't think it would have worked. I can't be too annoyed with my father. After all, he bought me the football annual and set me off on my football addiction.

My saviour through this difficult period of preadolescence was a man called Mr Gibson. He worked in a shop a few doors down from our house. He was an avid Wrexham fan who eventually twigged I'd never seen a professional match and offered to take me to watch Wrexham when they were at home to Exeter City in a Fourth Division fixture. My parents allowed me to go because the trip had been planned by 'nice Mr Gibson from the shop'. He parked the car in town and then we had a good ten-minute walk to the ground. I couldn't believe the number of people heading for the Racecourse. The crowd that day was 9,000 as Wrexham were pressing for promotion to the Third Division.

Outside the ground Mr Gibson and I went through different turnstiles. He told me to go into the boys' pen; then, at the final whistle, wait for him inside the ground and he'd find me. Once inside the pen I felt less like a herded sheep, which I have to say was the feeling I had outside the ground. I was hemmed in against some railings, before finding a gap, paying my money, and getting into the stadium.

Once inside the atmosphere was awe-inspiring. It took my breath away, made my whole body tingle. The noise was a torrent of chants and singing against a backdrop of babbling voices and chatter. The air was thick with the waft of cigarette smoke and the occasional cigar. Ahead of me, to the right and to the left, the terraces and stands were jam-packed. Never before had I seen so many people in one place. Had it not been for the safety of the boys' pen, I'd probably have been terrified. The noise was not just made by the crowd. In my section, several boys had what are now obsolete: football rattles. Others had klaxons which, when blown, sounded as if foghorns were sounding from ships run aground in the Racecourse stadium. I suppose in our Health and Safety obsessed world, even if a business tried to reintroduce football rattles, they'd be banned instantly. Heavy wooden contraptions, they made a piercing clanking noise which was probably over the government's decibel level. If an enthusiastic junior turned the handle too excitedly as Wrexham approached the goal, there was always the danger he'd be left holding the handle as the main structure flew through the air. This could result in hitting someone on the head, rendering them unconscious. I'm glad to report I never saw a Wrexham *Leader* headline stating, 'Death by Rattle at Home Match'.

KEEPING TABS ON OTHER MATCHES

At the bottom of each wall at the four corners of the ground were letters of the alphabet, with a gap between each letter. During the game I was to learn that these gaps would be filled with metal squares, each one bearing a painted number. The alphabet letters corresponded with those published in my football programme. For example, 'A' might be Arsenal v Spurs, and so on through the alphabet. At half-time someone would put numbers next to each letter. This meant that the crowd knew the scores at other grounds.

WREXHAM FC PREPARE ME FOR THE FUTURE

From my vantage point on the terraces it was like looking down on a green billiard table made of grass. Then the teams came out. The roar was so intense they must have heard it in my home village of Rhosllanerchrugog, four miles away.

From my reading, I knew my home team was doing well in the Fourth Division. So well that regular fans were convinced Wrexham would be promoted into the Third Division. They were playing well, but not on the day I watched them for the first time. As if to train me for a lifetime of cheering the Reds, members of the team decided to prepare me for the future by losing 1–2 to Exeter City.

When the final whistle blew some of the fans were

disappointed, and had their heads down with fixed glum faces. I was thrilled to have been in the atmosphere, even though we lost. There was far more on my mind than the result. I had to locate Mr Gibson. He'd obviously watched the game from another stand, as had hundreds if not thousands of others, who were now making their way to one of the few exits in the ground. The crowd that was pushing its way out, very near to where I had to stand, seemed to have its own momentum. Did all of them still have their feet on the ground I wondered, or were some of them semi-airborne? All the faces looked the same. Then I saw Mr Gibson's hand go up. I'd been hoping and praying he'd be very near to where I was standing. He wasn't. He was as far away as possible, without being outside the ground. As I was smaller than the men, I realised all I could do was dive in and hope that, with a variety of going through men's legs and general pushing, I'd get to Mr Gibson's hand. I felt like a non-swimmer heading for a boat out at sea. Eventually I was safe, and although there were still thousands of people on the road, I was relieved to breathe again. We walked towards town to pick up the car. On this, my first day at a professional football match, there was one other initiation ceremony. In Regent Street, scores of men gathered around the window of a TV shop. Several small screens were showing *Grandstand*, and at 5pm the results came up. Following a small team like Wrexham, many fans supported a big team as well. It was often a choice between Liverpool, Everton, Manchester United or Manchester City. For Wrexham fans it made sense to choose either Liverpool or Manchester United, as that way you could wear your red scarf and bobble hat if you were lucky enough to get to Anfield or Old Trafford. In the Sixties there wasn't the merchandise there is today, and scarves rarely had names on them.

In the car journey home Mr Gibson was very apologetic that my first game had been a defeat. He seemed to be worried I wouldn't want to go again. Nothing was further from the truth. I was hooked for life. There was, however, one thing bothering me. In the end I blurted it out.

'Mr Gibson, sometimes, please, could we go and watch Queens Park Rangers, because they're in the First Division?'

He looked startled. 'They play in London. That's hours away from here.'

'No, they're not,' I persisted, 'Queens Park is in Wrexham.'

On the outskirts of the town there was a council estate that bore that name. Reading my football books and magazines I'd imagined that somewhere, hidden in that labyrinth of streets, was a stadium housing a top team. Eventually I realised I'd got it wrong. Having delivered the thank you speech to Mr Gibson I'd been forced to rehearse several times before leaving the house, I returned home.

AFTER THE INITIATION

From then on I lived for when Saturday arrived. I attended a grammar school where most of the boys in my class supported big teams. I can't even say those early years as a Wrexham fan were a rollercoaster. It's more accurate to say that they were played out on a plateau of variable downs in a valley of mediocrity. Sometimes bearable, but more often than not unbearable. Once I was 14 my parents came to the realisation that they were never going to cure me of what was to them an unseemly addiction. So they grudgingly allowed me to go to games on my own, or with friends.

Despite my first game ending in a home defeat, my heroes in red rallied and played out a 0–0 draw with Colchester United towards the end of that season, which meant they were promoted to the heady heights of Division Three at the end of the 1961–62 season. I was chuffed. In my first season as their number one fan, my regular presence had inspired them and lifted them to the third tier. Thrilled by their promotion,

I had every intention of watching every future home game. With this success rate it would only take another two years of cheering to get the lads into the promised land of Division One, as the top tier was known in those days. Sadly, it only took two seasons for the harsh reality of being a football fan to take hold of me. Despite an encouraging finish of ninth, one season later Wrexham returned to the bottom division.

WHAT TO DO IF THERE'S NO FOOTBALL

With my team only playing on Saturdays and the occasional midweek match, it meant that there were six other days to fill. School took up a great part of them, as did sleep. Having totted up those commitments, I realised I was still left with 65 hours a week. How to fill them with football was a taxing problem. You must remember that this was in the dark ages before wall-to-wall TV coverage of games, or countless books covering every aspect of the beautiful game, and there certainly were no football blogs or highlights of games on YouTube. It was only possible to go out and kick a football with friends when the lighter nights or school holidays arrived.

In the privacy of my own bedroom I used to pretend I was a radio presenter. With a list of future fixtures before me, I would commentate on all the games Wrexham were due to play. Occasionally, some of the encounters were very close-fought affairs. The rest were easy victories for my team.

If what I've told you is slightly embarrassing, just you wait – you haven't heard anything yet! I got a large sheet of my mother's typing paper and drew a huge square. This square eventually played host to countless tiny squares. Into them I placed a number between nought and six, repeating the same individual numbers many times. Being aware that many games ended with low scores, I inserted many noughts and ones and was fairly sparse when distributing higher numbers such as four, five or six.

MY SUCCESSFUL TEAM

I was now ready to take Wrexham Football Club on its journey to world domination. It all started in the Fourth Division. Home and away fixtures against the other 23 clubs were listed. Then, with the large sheet of paper on my desk, I'd pick up the pen. Looking towards the ceiling, so as not to cheat, the nib would come down and land in one of the small boxes. Aldershot 0 Wrexham 2. An excellent start to the new campaign. You're probably wondering at what stage I started cheating. In fairness, I never cheated by looking down. I suppose what happened was that, as time went on, I became more and more aware of where certain numbers were positioned. It was probably this foresight which catapulted little Wrexham through the divisions at great speed, until they lifted the FA Cup and won the Division One championship in the same season. This magnificent feat was followed by a 4–1 romp against Inter Milan in the European Cup final. I could take you through the result of every individual match by consulting my exercise book, but unfortunately I no longer know where it is. I guess you're mightily relieved.

AFTER INTER, BACK TO REALITY

As I recount my years of following Wrexham, I have to point out I wasn't able to watch every game. There are two reasons for this. In the sixth form it was discovered I was an OK hockey goalie. The hockey master, a teacher called Selwyn Matthews, told me in his usual 'tell it as it is' way, that I was fairly unlikely to make it big in soccer as I was only average. If I'm not mistaken, the word 'rubbish' might even have popped up somewhere during his mini speech. From 1962 to the end of the 1968–69 season, I was a faithful attendee on the Wrexham terraces, initially spending my pocket money. Then, from 1964–69, I doled out some of my hard-earned paperboy money to make my way through the clanking, slightly terrifying sound of the turnstiles. It's more than likely that one of the reasons I stayed slim during my early teenage years was the fear of being stuck in the turnstiles during a game, or even for an entire season! To this day, despite my rapidly ascending age, I believe that once I've shown my ticket to the man in his box, I'm one of the fastest fans to get through the turnstiles.

It was just my luck that for the 1969–70 season I was often playing in a hockey goal on a Saturday. Sometimes I would make two appearances on the same day; for the school in the morning, then turning out for Monsanto Seconds in the afternoon. This was the season Wrexham returned to the Third Division. I saw some games, but also missed a lot. For four years until 1974 I was studying at Bangor University, playing hockey most Saturday afternoons. I did, however, manage to see some of Wrexham's European Cup heroics. FC Zürich had come out of the hat against us in the European Cup Winners' Cup, now called the UEFA Cup. In the Swiss newspapers the team's management had boasted they would probably stuff this unknown, unheard of Third Division outfit, 10–1. How wrong they were. We held them to a 1–1 draw at their stadium. In the return match at the Racecourse, I stood on the Kop behind the goal where Mel Sutton scored the winner in a 2–1 Wrexham victory. Along with 18,000 other fans, I jumped into the night air to celebrate our first-ever appearance and victory in that European competition.

When I finished university I got a teaching job in Eastham on the Wirral, and lived in Connah's Quay, just half an hour's drive from the Racecourse. Having stopped playing hockey, it meant that from 1974 until 1979 I was able to watch Wrexham on a regular basis. These were the golden years which culminated in them becoming Third Division champions in 1977–78 for the first time in their history. It also meant their first stay in the Second Division, now known as the Championship. It was such a joy to see teams like West Ham, Chelsea, Birmingham City and Leicester City roll up at the Racecourse to take on my home team, instead of the likes of Rochdale or Halifax. Sadly, their sojourn in the heady heights of the second tier didn't last long. Two successive relegations saw them back in the fourth tier by 1983.

LIFE AND WORK
GET IN THE WAY OF FOOTBALL

From 1979 until 2000 I lived and worked away from Wrexham, and lived in places as diverse as Leicester, Monmouth and Swansea, watching the 'lads' whenever I could if they played within a 40- or 50-mile radius of where I was living. This meant that, apart from the rare occasions I managed to get up to Wrexham, I saw them play mainly away from home. Of course they usually lost or, if I was lucky, snatched a draw. Very rarely would I drive back home to report a victory. Although, two famous matches stick in my memory. One was in the early Eighties when I was living and working in Leicester. Wrexham were in the third round of the FA Cup and were drawn away to Nottingham Forest who were managed by the legendary Brian Clough. It was 2 January 1982 when the game was finally played, having been postponed the day before because of thick fog. We were on a familiar route of sliding down the table and were living in the Second Division relegation zone. In 1979 and 1980 Forest had won the European Cup and, as a top team in the top tier, had some brilliant players. At half-time Forest were 1–0 in the lead and I was anticipating an onslaught from them in the second period. Instead, Wrexham scored three times, one of which came from the boot of Dixie McNeil, with Dowman and Vinter scoring the other two. At work in the Leicester office the following Monday, I enjoyed one of the best working days of my life. Many of the workers followed Forest. So, pretending not to know, and not letting on that I'd been at the match, I asked each one of them separately how Forest had got on against Wrexham. They all knew who I supported and eventually rumbled what I was doing. In spite of this, that particular workday was nearly as enjoyable as the afternoon I'd enjoyed at the ground.

The other not-to-be-forgotten moment was again in the third round of the FA Cup when I was living and working in Monmouth. On 4 January 1992, Wrexham faced yet another top team from the top division at home. Arsenal were 0–1 up at half-time, seemingly coasting to victory. That was still the situation with just eight minutes to go. Then Mickey Thomas took one of the greatest free kicks he struck in his life. England's goalkeeper David Seaman had absolutely no chance of stopping it. It was 1–1 and we all thought we'd be booking trips to Highbury to watch the replay. Local boy Steve Watkin had other ideas and, two minutes later, after receiving the ball from Gordon Davies, he wriggled and wormed his way past defenders in the penalty box to score the winner, 2–1 to Wrexham. Cue the final whistle, followed by a pitch invasion. Wrexham fans painted the town red that night and copious streams of alcohol flowed through the streets into the next morning.

In 1993 we were promoted to the third tier and relegated in 2002–03. We bounced back up, then straight back down, and it was all downhill after that. In 2004 the club went into administration, and then in 2008 we were relegated into non-league and have been there ever since. In April 2011 the club was given a winding-up order. They had one day to find the final £100,000 of the £250,000 they owed to the Inland Revenue. Fans rallied to the cause, including a man who mortgaged his house, and a ten-year-old boy, at the front of the queue, who had emptied his savings book to give all that he'd saved to the club.

ROCKBOTTOM FOOTBALL - FOOTBALL AS WE'VE NEVER SEEN IT BEFORE

I moved back to live in Wrexham permanently in 2010. I decided to watch Wrexham as often as I could. This decision was born out of duty rather than desire. The fans had saved a club that meant so much to me. It was time to bury any thoughts of watching nearby Premiership teams.

Carrying out my pledge has not been easy. Many times at the final whistle I have turned to a person sitting next to me and said, 'That's it. I really can't watch this standard of football any more.' Whoever I've been sitting next to always says, 'See you at the next home game in a fortnight's time.' They're always right. Always, at the next game, I'm there. There's no psychologist in the land capable of curing this obsession that has pursued and defined me for so many years.

In the years of non-league football, when watching my team struggle to defeat the likes of Dover Athletic, it's been painful to remember that this is the club who, in the past, has caused Cup sensations against great sides. Once, in a pub in Windsor, I got talking to a Portuguese tourist. When he discovered I was a Wrexham fan his face clouded over. All his life he'd followed Porto. Somehow, he guessed I was going to berate him with the tale of one of Wrexham's greatest European exploits. And, of course, he was right.

In the autumn of 1984, when Wrexham were near the bottom of the Fourth Division, they were drawn against Porto, one of the top teams in Europe. Miraculously, Wrexham won the first leg 1–0 at the Racecourse. We Wrexham fans are very confident when predicting defeats. We're never so confident about potential victories. For the trip to Portugal we were all rock solid in our belief that we'd get a massive pasting. With not long to go, we were trailing 4–1. (At least our opponents didn't really have enough time to score another six before the final whistle – that was some consolation.)

Then the unthinkable happened. We scored twice to lose 4–3, which meant that over the two matches we'd drawn 4–4, and because of the away goals ruling we went through, having knocked out the mighty Porto. After reliving the events of those two nights for my new friend from Porto, he looked more crestfallen and depressed than when I'd started the story. Needless to say, he didn't buy me a drink and he left the bar quite quickly.

It was not just against Porto that Wrexham shone in the European Cup Winners' Cup. We could also boast almost beating Anderlecht in the season that the Belgian giants went on to win the final against West Ham. In the Eighties the crack Spanish side, Real Zaragoza, were held to a 0–0 draw at their ground. At a rocking, raucous Racecourse, we drew 2–2 in the home tie and this time it was our turn to go out because of the away goals rule. Sadly, in the Nineties, any chance of more great European triumphs was curtailed when the Welsh FA ruled that Welsh clubs playing in the English leagues would no longer be allowed access to Europe.

And it was not just in European competitions that Wrexham showed their giant-killing abilities. We have already noted the humbling of top teams such as Nottingham Forest and Arsenal. In my time following the Reds, I can recall the humbling of quite a few top-tier teams by Wrexham when they were either in the third or fourth tier. Newcastle United, Sunderland, Southampton, Bristol City, all spring to mind as other FA Cup conquests, while there were also League Cup victories over Leicester City and a magnificent 2–3 away victory at White Hart Lane against a strong Tottenham Hotspur side.

IT CAN ONLY GET BETTER, AND IT COULD BE WORSE

On an April evening in 2008, the unthinkable happened. Wrexham, who had been an English Football League club for 87 years, were relegated after losing 2–0 at Hereford's Edgar Street ground. Brian Little, a top manager, who'd enjoyed success with Aston Villa, had replaced Brian Carey in November 2007, but was unable to save Wrexham. It meant that for the 2008–09 season, Wrexham were in the Blue Square League (now called the Vanarama National League). In other words, after all the glories of the Seventies, they were now a non-league club playing in the fifth tier of football.

The only ray of sunshine for fans is that there were other teams who were in a worse position. If you don't believe me just try and imagine being a Fort William fan in the Highland League in Scotland. They ended their last full season just before Covid closed football down. In that season, 2018–19, they finished 18th, bottom. They played 34 games and lost 32. Many of them were by margins of ten goals or more, and a couple of times they were stuffed 14–1. Although they managed two draws and no wins, they still finished the season on –7 points due to fielding ineligible players on three separate occasions. Their derby rivals are 66 miles away in Clachnacuddin. When Fort William secured their first point against their greatest rivals, with a 3–3 draw, they made BBC Radio news headlines. That night, after the match, the celebrations flowed into the wee small hours of the next day. Being placed in such a difficult location, high in the uplands of Scotland, lots of their games are postponed because of bad weather. The most spectacular postponement was because of deer droppings on the pitch!

For us Wrexham fans, it's difficult to believe – but it really could be worse than languishing in the fifth tier!

LIVING THE NIGHTMARE

Brian Little, despite his exploits with top teams such as Aston Villa, had overseen our demise into non-league football. The opening game of our life in non-league saw us thrash Stevenage Borough, 5–1. At the final whistle, the Wrexham faithful filed out of the ground full of hope. This was going to be easy. Come next May, we'd be back in the English Football League where we belonged.

How wrong could they be? Fifteen years on, at the beginning of 2023, we were still a fifth tier, non-league outfit.

Brian Little was not the only one to take the manager's seat with his and the fans optimism high at the start of his tenure. The list contains 14 names. These can all say, 'I came, I saw, I conked out,' to misquote Emperor Julius Caesar. Dean Saunders, Andy Morrell, Billy Barr, Kevin Wilkin, Carl Darlington, Gary Mills, Dean Keates (twice), Andrew Davies, Sam Ricketts, Graham Barrow, Bryan Hughes, Brian Flynn. In fairness, one or two of them were in a caretaker role while the board were looking for a successor. Carl Darlington, for example, sat in the hot seat for only three days.

With all of those memories of huge crowds and staggering victories, you can understand why it's not quite so exhilarating to watch the likes of Braintree grinding their way through their game plan. Incidentally, for that game the away side brought 13 fans. That was clearly a minibus job for some Essex driver. Just three short of Weymouth in 2021, who must have hired a slightly larger vehicle for their 16 fans.

Before Wrexham slid through the trap-door into non-league football, almost all the teams they encountered had a previous rich footballing heritage. Along with Wrexham there are 11 other teams in their division with a history of exploits in the English Football League. Clubs such as Notts County, Southend United, Grimsby Town, Chesterfield, Halifax Town, Dagenham & Redbridge, Yeovil Town,

Aldershot, Barnet, Maidstone United, Oldham Athletic, Scunthorpe United. But what can one say about Maidenhead or Kings Lynn? Maidenhead is part of the Royal Borough of Windsor and Maidenhead. Do the royal family support them? If they took all their auxiliary staff, such as toothpaste squeezers and others, along to matches, it really would swell their attendance. Kings Lynn, which also sounds regal and historical, has very little to boast about, apart from the fact that it's the most dangerous medium-sized town in Norfolk, and is among the top 20 most dangerous overall, out of Norfolk's 546 towns, villages and cities...

CHAPTER 2

RUMBLINGS
AND RUMOURS

AFTER 13 SEASONS of substandard football, in the 2020–21 season rumours started circulating the streets and bars of the town that someone famous wanted to buy the club. Not just one person – but two famous individuals.

In early 2020 Wrexham director Spencer Harris was approached by an intermediary about a potential change in the ownership of the club. In the summer of that year Harris and his fellow directors agreed to sign a non-disclosure agreement with the interested parties.

It was not long before these two unknown individuals fuelled the rumour mill, with Wrexham fans overactive in trying to work out their identities. People assumed it would be people with a strong connection to the club. Was one of them Mark Hughes, born and bred in Ruabon just six miles outside the town? Or how about Robbie Savage, born in Bradley, a village outside Wrexham, or maybe even Mickey Thomas, who had played for the club and gone into the annals of history for his super strike against Arsenal? And so it went on and on, with more names being bandied around, accompanied with more and more certainty from fans convinced that they had the facts.

In our wildest dreams, we Wrexham fans would never have guessed that two Hollywood stars were bidding for the club:

Ryan Reynolds of *Deadpool* film fame, and Rob McElhenney, star of *It's Always Sunny in Philadelphia*.

Members of Wrexham FC were asked to vote on the matter. In September 2020 they were asked whether they would authorise discussions with potential new owners. Of the 2,108 fans qualified to vote, only 31 said 'no'. This meant that the interested parties were asked to put a deal on the table which the fans could vote on in November 2020. In that vote, only 29 voted 'no'.

While I was pleased with the result, I understood the views of those who preached caution and voted 'no'. The Supporters Trust had done a superb job in rescuing the club, and although the atmosphere behind the scenes had apparently become toxic, they must still be praised for the work they did. Some 'no' voters also felt they had seen all this before at other clubs. High-profile names taking over, then abandoning a club when it was almost on its knees. Of course, Wrexham fans had seen it all before too. We'll never forget the exploits of Messers Hamilton and Guterman who took the club into administration.

Issue one of the glitzy Wrexham fanzine, *Fearless in Devotion*, carried an article entitled 'Minority Report... why we voted "no".' The editors spoke to three of the 29 who voted against the takeover. One received vitriolic responses after stating on Facebook that s/he was thinking of voting against the takeover. All three agreed that fans' ownership, for whatever reason, had become toxic and, in their opinion, this had opened the door to talk of a takeover. They were also disappointed and horrified by the abuse Spencer Harris and manager Dean Keates had received from many Wrexham fans. In their opinion, poor on-field displays by the team and bad decisions off the field had contributed to the inevitability of new ownership. They also felt it was more or less impossible to have a balanced decision about the takeover when the potential new owner, Ryan Reynolds, was handing out bottles of gin to some fans. The three were convinced that, in the future, the day would come when the two megastars would move on and the fans would have to be ready to pick up the pieces and start all over again.

The new owners were certainly quick to engage with fans. Not for them the cold wave of a new owner to the fans at a first home match. Very quickly they linked with the Wrexham faithful. Having been informed about a Wrexham family who were fanatic followers of the team, Rob and Ryan sent them £6,000. This paid for essential alterations to the house which were necessary to help one of their children who was disabled.

Ryan Reynolds stated: 'We want to be at the Racecourse Ground as much as possible – as many games as I can make. We want to have a drink with the fans. You'll be fed up with us.' They also endeared themselves by stating that, in taking over the club, they were to be guided by four main principles:

- To protect the heritage of the club
- Not change, but reinforce the values of how it's woven into the town itself
- Use their own resources to grow the club so that it had a global appeal
- Reward the fans

A STRANGE SEASON BEGINS

It was the start of the 2020–21 season, and hopes among Wrexham fans were, as always, lowest of the low. Sorry if you were expecting me to drop in the word 'high' somewhere. But it would be misleading and I'd be lying. There were two main reasons. First, in the previous season, my beloved team had finished just one point above the relegation zone. A couple fewer points would have brought the ignominy of this once proud club slipping out of the Vanarama National League into the Vanarama North – the same league as Chester, our great rivals. In all the years I've followed Wrexham, if we have failed to win anything, the all-important quest is to make sure we finish higher than the local enemy. Second, with Covid holding its grip on most of the UK, the new season didn't start until October (instead of the usual August kick-off). In addition, fans were not allowed into stadia. The only way of watching was to pay my £10 and sit glued to a laptop every Saturday afternoon.

FOOTBALL STREAMING, ME SCREAMING!

It all sounds so easy. But not for me. I'm a world champion techno idiot. While I'd surprised myself and close friends by being able to get on to Zoom for some meetings, and even started online banking, I'm dwelling on my meagre successes and hiding the embarrassing failures. Some of these were quite spectacular. Top of the poll, or should that be pole – the slippery one – goes to my appearance on the first-ever meeting of the newly-formed North Wales Society of Authors. I was due to lead the discussion on what we all wanted from the group. All they got were fleeting images of a bright orange digital me. From time to time, flashes of my fleeting shape across their screens were accompanied by statements, most of which were totally incoherent. It's incredible what technology can do to me even without the influence of alcohol.

Having abandoned my appearances at the Authors online meetings, I concentrated my electronic efforts on watching Wrexham FC matches streamed. At the beginning this met with mixed levels of success. Eventually, the games got better and better in terms of visual accuracy on my screen. I suppose it was because I was getting better at finding my way to the virtual seat every week, plus the fact that the cameraman was finally winning his battles against bad angles.

The opening game of the season was a victory over Boreham Wood who looked like a good side and much better than us. You'll be relieved to know that I'm not going through the season, game by game. Otherwise, by now, you would have worked out that there are another 43 to go. I will however mention a 0–0 home draw against Halifax in the same season. I made notes as the game unfolded, if that's the right word to use. Unfolded suggests action and commitment. There was little evidence of either. The commentator was being very kind to Wrexham and claimed we were probably struggling because we have such a wide pitch. The truth is, we can struggle on any surface.

I began to wonder why the whole experience looked so poor on the laptop. The cameraman wasn't keeping up with the plot. Crosses, corners, throw-ins came from invisible players hiding in the corners of my screen. When I pressed the arrow to lengthen or broaden the screen, I ended up with an advert for controlling haemorrhoids. Five minutes before half-time I risked it, and lost the picture completely!

Once I got the picture back and the game returned to my living room I began to wonder whether Wrexham had signed up to another league. It looked like they were now playing a game called three passes. The idea was that on the third pass you gave the ball to the opposition. It's like a bizarre version of rugby league for footballers.

Because of Covid there were no fans in the ground. No Energy. No Passion. Dean Keates, the manager, stood on the touchline looking as if he was waiting for a train. I began to miss all the things that accompanied watching football in the past. The smell of hot dogs, fighting the eye-stinging pungency of onions. The throbbing pubs before and after the match.

I missed the talk of people I don't know. Although unknown, they shared a common goal with me. We could all talk together about football without the glazed look of partners asking if there was anything good on another channel.

I even missed the sandwich board man, who in the days before all-seater stadia used to walk up and down the terraces holding aloft a board on which there was a text from the Bible. At one game, we were 0–1 down to Sheffield Wednesday after a howler of a mistake by our goalie. The text broadcast the fact, JESUS CHRIST, HE WILL SAVE US. 'Well stick him in goal then,' shouted a fan standing near me.

As the game between Wrexham and Halifax tries to crank into some kind of second-half action, I wonder if I'd be better off not paying for this twice weekly 'home' match on my laptop. After all, I could stay at home, depress myself just as successfully without watching the match (having shelled out £10).

Christmas has gone but we are still in need of New Year saviours. Although the fans have said they want Rob and Ryan at the helm, we are still waiting for everything to be signed and sealed. In the past I enjoyed the day out even if the game was dire. That's much more difficult in my living room. Even with an open bottle of red wine next to my screen, I'm desperately missing the banter with other fans. I've tried talking to the cat who's watching the game with me. Didn't work. No response. With supporters I remember all the great moves, cracking shots, spectacular saves, the ball shaking or shaving posts. With this awful performance I might just recall the fouls – there are so many of them. Even the tomcat scratches the door anxious to get out. This is a bore too far, even for a tomcat used to spending hour after hour of his life doing nothing more than licking himself.

The final whistle brings the curtain down on a truly dreadful game. The manager appears to smile at the fact we have achieved another clean sheet. Will someone please tell him he's running a football club not a hotel?

THE TWO MAIN ACTORS
IN WREXHAM'S NEW ADVENTURE

Tuesday, 9 February 2021, will always remain an important day in the minds of most Wrexham fans. This is the day when the anxieties of will they, won't they, are finally laid to rest. It was on this day everything was cleared and Ryan and Rob finally signed on the dotted line as co-owners of Wrexham Football Club. The team, under the management of Dean Keates, celebrated by beating Altrincham 1–2 away.

Thrilled that things were now going to move forward, and that in the future money would be available to buy decent players, I indulged in football fantasising of my own.

TWO SUPERSTARS AT THE HELM

As noted, Ryan is famous for his role in *Deadpool*, while Rob stars in the sitcom *It's Always Sunny in Philadelphia*. I wondered whether there were any elements of those scripts we could foresee creeping into the way Wrexham would be run in the future? In *Deadpool*, Wilson, the main character played by Ryan Reynolds, ends up in a spot of bother when he makes fun of his main rival, Ajax, on discovering that his real name is Francis. As punishment, his enemy puts him in a hyperbaric chamber that periodically takes Wilson (Ryan Reynolds) to the verge of asphyxiation, over a weekend. Well, perhaps not. Surely, not even the most ardent Wrexham fan would wish that kind of experience on a Chester fan.

So what about Rob's sitcom? Similar result I'm afraid. The series follows the exploits of 'The Gang', a group of narcissistic friends who run an Irish bar in Philadelphia. They will do anything to get what they want and feel no shame about doing what others would find despicable. The following are chosen at random from previous episodes, and I suppose you could say they are just for starters! A small sample of what the gang have got up to include: becoming addicted to crack cocaine and pretending to be mentally challenged in order to qualify for welfare support; attempted cannibalism and kidnapping; hiding naked inside a couch to eavesdrop on other people; impersonating police officers to get free goods and extort civilians. Should I go on? I could. There's plenty more where all that came from, but I won't. It's so good that, outside acting, Rob and Ryan are really nice guys.

ANY CHANCE OF LOST IN TRANSLATION?

As I look forward to Ryan and Rob playing a major part in the development of my club, I begin to wonder whether there will be language difficulties for them. I realise English is spoken both sides of the Pond. But. And there is a but. Interesting that I've fastened onto that word at the beginning of my thoughts. In America, but means backside and, of course, we all know the meaning of the word here in Britain. A friend of mine, who was involved in running a theological college for future ministers and vicars, once told me this story.

The college was contacted by the Southern Baptists asking for a British student to go on a preaching tour of some of their churches. The principal, realising how strict and serious the denomination was, decided to send a very serious student.

Terry, that's what we'll call him, arrived in the United States totally unaware that, to the Americans, saying 'but' signified someone's backside. He began his talk: 'I'm delighted to be here and I want to talk to you about the Christian "But".' He obviously intended to draw attention to the idea that Christians often pledge to do this or that, but never do it because they come up with all kinds of excuses.

Terry continued, 'I have three points. First, every Christian has a but. Second, my but will be different to your but, and thirdly, in the bonds of Christian fellowship we must learn to

31

share each other's but.' I could tell you the response, but I'll leave it to your imagination.

In our country a banger is eaten with mashed potatoes whereas in America it's a beat-friendly song. There could also be confusion if braces are mentioned. Here they bolster difficult teeth, whereas in the States they hold up trousers. In the States a chippie is a woman of loose morals, whereas in Britain it's where we get our fish and chips or faggots and peas, or whatever ticks the culinary box.

There are quite a few other examples of potential embarrassment. In the following list I'll mention the English meaning first, then what the word signifies in the States:

HOOKER – a position in rugby union / a prostitute
AA – Alcoholics Anonymous / American Airlines
JUMPER – garment worn over a shirt / someone
    committing suicide
HAMPER – food basket for picnics / basket for dirty
    washing
QUEEN –sovereign leader / transvestite
BOSS – manager / cool, awesome
BUM – buttocks / hobo, homeless person
HOO-HA – female genitalia / argument
HOOTER – siren / female breasts
NHS – National Health Service / National Honour
    Society
BOOTY – treasure / female buttocks

I could have waxed eloquently on the potential gaffes between the words in the various doublings, but again I will let you create your own embarrassing situations.

My sister lived for many years in America, so I visited several times and became very fond of the States. Dining in a restaurant, I asked the waiter whether it would be possible to have a jacket potato with my salad. A little later he returned looking somewhat flummoxed. 'I've asked everyone in the kitchens and no one has a clue as to the meaning of a jacket potato. And I'm keen to know if, in England, your potatoes sometimes wear suits?'

On one of my early visits I ordered chips with my medium-rare steak. That was the day I learned that chips mean crisps in America. Crisps accompanied my steak and salad.

My sister invited a friend of hers for an evening meal. I picked up the phone to hear the friend explain, 'I'm really sorry, I'll have to blow off this evening.' One of the meanings of that phrase in Britain is 'to fart'. I was amazed that she knew what effect my sister's culinary efforts would have on her, before seeing what was on the menu even. In the States the phrase is used to explain that the caller will have to drop out of an engagement.

The reign of Ryan and Rob will bring much fun and laughter and, as we've seen, there could be a few word gaffes too, on both sides, but I'm sure we'll all get along just fine.

LET THE IMAGINATION RUN RIOT

Another fantasy about the takeover picks up on Ryan and Rob's stated vision to make Wrexham a global force in the world of football. Perhaps it's time to reintroduce my schoolboy pencil, pricking the sheet of paper and creating scores. As already noted, Wrexham humbled Inter Milan 4–1 in the European champions' final with just a couple of pricks. Who knows, perhaps our film stars can lead us to that glory too. Before every home match the Wrexham players run out to a version of 'Men of Harlech'. The words were rewritten in the Seventies during the team's heyday:

> Here they come our mighty champions,
> Raise your voices to the anthem,
> Marching like a mighty army,
> Wrexham is the name.

See the Reds who fight together,
Speak their names with pride for ever,
Marching like a mighty army,
Wrexham is the name.

Fearless in devotion. Rising to promotion,
Rising to the ranks of mighty heroes,
Fighting foes in every land,
History only tells a story,
We are here to see your glory,
Stand aside, the Reds are coming,
Wrexham is the name.

We have made the mighty humble,
We have made the mountains tumble,
Falling to a mighty army Wrexham is the name.

I must admit that in the last 15 seasons I've often been too embarrassed to sing those stirring sentiments, especially when the crowd belts out, 'Rising to promotion.' Really? My lips struggle to send those words into the atmosphere. So often I've been expected to sing them in the aftermath of being humbled by the likes of Braintree or Dover. But now, with the two Hollywood boys in charge and money available to buy players, too hot for most Vanarama defences to handle, who knows? Who knows?

While I'm in fantasy mode, dwelling on global supremacy, there are plenty of dreams keen to break out.

- I see young boys begging their football-loving fathers to take them to watch Wrexham rather than Liverpool or Man City.
- Wrexham are regularly on *Match of the Day*: at the beginning of the programme, not the last featured match before we all turn out the lights for the night. During the programme Gary Lineker gets endless tweets from fans in Llanfair Caereinion, Rhosllanerchrugog and Llanfairpwllgwyngyllgogerwchwyrndrobwllllantysilio

gogogoch claiming Wrexham is a brilliant Premiership team.

- An airport is built near the town to satisfy the demand for flights from fans from all over the world keen to see Wrexham pit their wits against top sides.
- Ryan considers putting himself forward for the team, while fans clamour for our six-foot-six chairman, Humphrey Ker, to go in goal.
- The Pope asks for an audience with Rob and Ryan.
- Deadpool Lager is launched despite the fact that some dissenting voices suggest Dead Cool sounds more appetising. Sixty-three per cent of Wrexham children, boys and girls, when asked, 'What do you want to do when you grow up?', reply 'Play for Wrexham, of course.'

CHAPTER 3

THE 2020-21 SEASON IN A NUTSHELL

I'VE ALREADY COVERED the Halifax game of 26 January 2021 in all its lurid glory. Or should that be drudgery? In addition, you are aware that we won our first game against Boreham Wood (2–1) against the run of play. Despite two wins in our opening four, it was probably watching the fifth game that 'fan's despair' broke out all over my body and mind. We were away to Wealdstone, who were newly-promoted to the Vanarama National League and, up until that Saturday, had not won a game.

As usual for that season, Covid stipulated that the game had to be watched on my computer. It was up to me to create the atmosphere. Although I've got a loud voice when I concentrate and project it, even I struggled to create the volume of 3,000 or so individuals. In spite of this problem, I think I did pretty well on the number of expletives uttered in 90 minutes. In the opening 15 minutes two things struck me. Firstly, Wealdstone weren't very good. That was no great shock. After all, since returning to my home town in 2010, I had seen 20-odd opposition teams each year and knew the vast majority veered from dire to really dire. However, the 15th minute became the head-in-hands minute, as Wealdstone took the lead. That moment of utter depression was followed by six frenzied minutes of joy, as Wrexham scored twice to nudge ahead 1–2, but then Jacob Mendy equalised for the home side. I enjoyed my half-time drink, though the atmosphere at the bar left a lot to be desired. My glass of red was imbibed alone, staring at a frozen screen. In spite of being level, I was confident we were strong enough to beat them in the second half. My certainty lasted just 35 minutes, or if you throw in half-time as well, I was in football heaven for a total of 50 minutes. Then, between the 57th and 63rd minute, Wealdstone scored twice to go 4–2 ahead. The Reds scored in the last minute of normal time, but were unable to level the scores in added time.

At the final whistle there was still some alcohol left in the bottle, so I negotiated a free transfer to my glass. As I pondered the defeat, I realised that commentary and expert analysis on the Wrexham streaming service is often far better than at some of the other grounds. On that front, Wealdstone had certainly excelled in mediocrity, with expert analysis coming from a Wealdstone FC legend who I'd never heard of. Unlike the likes of Brian Laws and Andy Morrell, who stream regularly for Wrexham, Mr Wealdstone didn't appear to know the identity of the players in front of him. One thing he obviously didn't have in front of him was a team sheet. He referred to most of them as 'that player whose name I don't know' or the 'number 7, was it?', or 'perhaps number 8. Sorry I can't remember.' I'm also very sorry. Not sorry I can't remember their names, but deeply sorry I can remember most of the 90 minutes.

The season grinded on in the usual up and down way, with some good performances matched by desperate results. In our familiar pattern, we were occasional stalkers around the top spot. We could never be arrested for it, because we never stayed there long enough to be noticed. Instead, we flattered to deceive by hovering in and out of the play-off positions.

Although we were regular visitors in that terrain, since 2008 those visits had always failed to deliver the result which we all craved. Defeats in the play-offs to Luton home and away, plus a home loss to Eastleigh, still smart. Of course, as a Welsh fan, I will never forget the defeat to Newport County in the Wembley play-off final. That result's particularly hard to swallow as, just a couple of months before, we'd made our first appearance on the hallowed turf against Grimsby Town in the FA Trophy final. Having won that on penalties, I suppose we returned to the stadium feeling we belonged there and that we'd make the long journey back to north Wales with two trophies in the bag. As you and I now know, that was not to be.

Turning back to the 2020–21 season, on 9 February, there was a significant match away to Altrincham. It was played on the day that Rob and Ryan officially became owners of Wrexham FC. Unlike my first day of being linked to the club as a besotted fan, when I was welcomed with a 1–2 home defeat, they were rewarded with a 1–2 away win, with Kwame Thomas getting both the goals.

Apart from Hollywood stars becoming Wrexham owners, there is one other quirky piece of information from that day. One member of the squad for that match did not join his fellow players at the Racecourse ahead of the game to make the journey to Altrincham. Despite his failure to turn up, he still played. Just in case this ever comes up at one of your pub quizzes, I'll resolve the riddle for you. Christian Dibble lives very near Alty's ground.

As an incentive to the players, a couple of weeks after taking over Rob and Ryan announced that the players were on a bonus for each game for the rest of the season. They would have £200 extra in their wages for every win, and £50 for every draw. When I learned about this incentive, it reminded me of Crewe Alexandra. They once came up with a bonus scheme through which one lucky striker in the squad could end up with a brand-new car. All he had to do was score 30 or more goals in the 1982–83 season. No one got anywhere near the target. Further investigation assured me that the local garage's offer was always going to be safe. In the previous season the entire squad had only managed to amass 29 goals between them.

Two games after the Altrincham triumph, Wrexham visited Aldershot. In a world of new football stadia all looking the same, it's always a joy to go to the Shots' Recreation Ground. You walk through a park to get to the ground. I suppose that's why, way back in history, they gave it the imaginative name of the Recreation Ground. The first time I saw a game there, I remember a ball boy having to climb a tree to retrieve one of the footballs. Earlier I used the word joy to describe visits to their ground. Of course, in February 2021, we were all still in lockdown so I could only watch the match online. Wrexham were so awful that Rob and Ryan's extra bonus money was never at risk. After the half-time break, Wrexham players took an eternity to surface and I wondered if they'd done the honest thing and jumped back on the bus and gone back home. A 3–0 defeat was so comprehensive against a toothless side, that, in true fan fashion, I began to wonder whether this team would be capable of winning another game. Fortunately, the lure of bonus cash kicked in and we were undefeated in the next five games, winning four and drawing one. Once again the fans, including myself, were convinced that we were going to make it to the play-offs and we'd finally win a play-off final, and march into the long sealed-off promised land of League Two. Then, three games against teams all challenging at the top of the table burst the optimistic bubble. Two 1–0 defeats against Notts County (A) and Torquay (H) and a 3–0 thumping at Edgeley Park at the hands of Stockport County brought us all back down to earth. These teams all looked good enough to be in the English Football League, whereas we looked average. Another season of Vanarama drudgery beckoned. But wait, my doubting heart! Two staggering 0–4 wins away from home against Halifax and Woking got our pulses racing again. Those two victories heralded the start of an unbeaten run of five wins and two draws. After a 0–1 defeat at home to Notts County, and a pulsating 5–3 victory over Kings Lynn, we were in the play-offs and just needed to win our last match against Dagenham & Redbridge to ensure our place in the play-offs. In fact, in the last ten games of the season, we'd won six, drawn three, and just lost that one game against Notts County.

LAST CHANCE SALOON

On that last Saturday of the season, the government allowed certain teams to welcome fans back into their grounds after the lockdown regulations. One thousand one hundred and fifty-eight Dagenham fans turned up. Sadly, Wrexham were not able to take their fans with them.

As the game started streaming, Wrexham fans or those listening to it on the radio had eyes or ears on what was happening at matches in places far away from Kent. At kick-off, Wrexham needed to win to make the play-offs. Surely, even erratic, unpredictable Wrexham could do that, especially after their impressive run at the end of the season. Five teams, Chesterfield, Bromley, Wrexham, Eastleigh and Halifax were all fighting for two play-off places – to be sixth or seventh in the table.

There is something you need to know about Wrexham. If the papers and the press say they don't have a snowball's chance in hell of winning, that normally rouses them to memorable exploits and a great victory. On the other hand, if everyone anticipates they should have a comfortable passage, that inspires them to turn in a truly woeful performance. Which is precisely what they did in those first dire 45 minutes. Despite playing as if this was a training match rather than the most vital encounter of the season, at half-time the match was all-square and goalless. Because of events at the other grounds, when the teams came out for the second half we were still in sixth position and heading for the play-offs. I can't say that hope was springing eternally in my heart, it's more accurate to say there was a gentle flutter of possibility. Surely, Dean Keates would have laid into them, telling them they just had to get a grip and go for it. I didn't care what words he used. Expletives were totally acceptable as long as they had the desired effect. I was certain of one thing. Their performance could not possibly be as bad as it was in the first half. It wasn't. It was worse.

Dreams of a last-day win, followed by a breathtaking victory at Wembley after disposing of someone else, were destroyed early on when Paul Rutherford was sent off. A few minutes later it got worse when McCallum scored. Despite Ponticelli's last-gasp equaliser to give us a 1–1 draw, Ben Williamson's goal for Bromley at home to Notts County meant they leapfrogged us. Chesterfield did exactly the same at Halifax, where Nathan Tyson's late winner gave them a 1–2 win. We finished eighth with 68 points. The end of another season, where we had flattered to deceive. A local barman once told me the surprising fact that his pub sold more drinks when Wrexham lost than when they won. Whether there was much alcohol drunk that night in Wrexham, I've no idea. I, for one, had little or no taste for the stuff, and spent the evening staring mutely at the TV. What was being served up on the screen was just as bad, if not worse, than my team's performance.

WILL IT STILL BE DEANO?

So that's where we found ourselves, us Wrexham fans, staring into the barrel of mediocrity with another season in the Vanarama National League beckoning. I know, I know. Even if we'd beaten Dagenham, the chances were that we wouldn't have made it to the Wembley final and then League Two. While I know that, I'm sure you realise by now that our staple diet as Wrexham fans is, 'What if?'

The nagging fear in fans' minds was, would Ryan and Rob think Dean Keates had done a good job and keep him as manager. He had certainly bigged up his ambition in an earlier interview with the *Evening Leader*:

> I twice took a club on in a relegation-threatened season, brought my own players in, we have gelled them and we have been disciplined. This season we have been effective, we are in the top-five goal scorers. Would I like to get that opportunity? Of course I would. A few additions with the extra money that is coming in. I wouldn't say it is far off. The owners will make a decision that they feel is right for their football club.

Many fans spent the 2020–21 season attacking him on Facebook and wherever else they could get their voice heard. Many of them found it impossible to forgive him for leaving the club in 2018–19, with just six games remaining. We were in a strong position for the play-offs and Keates went off to manage Walsall, his childhood team. Andy Davies took charge to the end of the season, and he lost all but one game, so we missed out on the play-offs. It's strange to hear the manager say what a great job he'd done, especially when he had taken over a relegation-threatened side. He seemed to ignore the fact that, in the season he returned, he turned us into a relegation side so that, when the Covid lockdown kicked in and caused the abrupt curtailment of the season, we were just one point above the relegation zone.

Fans didn't have to agonise too long over the question, 'Will he stay or will he go?' Two days after the Dagenham debacle we got the answer as newspaper headlines proclaimed 'Keates gets axe'.

Rob and Ryan stated in the *Evening Leader*, 31 May 2021:

We would like to thank Dean, Andy and Karl for all their efforts on behalf of the club, in what at times were challenging circumstances. We are committed to returning the club to the EFL at the earliest opportunity, and feel that a change of manager will provide us with the best chance of achieving that objective. Dean, Andy and Karl will always be welcome at the Club.

'Will they?' I ask myself.

CHAPTER 4

WHO'D BE A MANAGER?

WHEN A CLUB announces that it's looking for a manager, very quickly those with pedigree, despite the fact that they've been sacked several times by different clubs, announce they're available and slam in their CVs. Alongside these acceptable overtures, most clubs also receive approaches from lifelong fans. Their experience usually consists of having watched *Match of the Day* since its first transmission in the Sixties. Or, if they're younger, since they learned to feed themselves with the full range of cutlery.

Some years ago, during the last home game of the season, the Spurs manager did something totally unexpected in the last ten minutes. All season he'd endured the loud comments of a fan telling him what he should do. In the final minutes he came out of the dugout and invited the vociferous critic to swap places with him. My guess is that the manager was as shocked as the rest of the onlookers when the 'know it all' accepted his invitation. I suppose all us fans are guilty of thinking we know what should be done at our club. A quick glance at fans' sites proves that.

In a similar vein a female journalist, who knew nothing about football and had never been to a match, was sent by her editor to watch a professional game, then write a report. When she returned to the office she shared her amazement at what she'd experienced. She was unable to understand why it was that the only people who didn't know what they were doing were the 22 players on the field, plus the manager and coaching staff. By contrast, all the people watching from the stands knew exactly what the players should be doing. She wondered why some of them were not swapped with the hapless and hopeless professionals out on the field.

I resisted the temptation to send in one of those crackpot applications. Although, I suppose, I could have mentioned I'd led Wrexham to glory in the European final with that famous 4–1 victory over Inter Milan. Sadly, it wouldn't have taken the interview panel too long to realise the victory had been off the field rather than on it, with a pencil and a piece of paper.

HOW LONG WILL THIS ONE LAST?

In our throwaway society, once we've bought a new mobile phone or computer we're immediately wondering about the next one. How can we improve on what we've just bought? It's very much like that with football managers. Of course it wasn't always that way. According to David Pickering's *Cassell Soccer Companion*, at Celtic, Willie Maley was in the hot seat for 50 years, right up until the Second World War. Charles Foweraker managed Bolton Wanderers for 25 years, while Eric Taylor was at the helm at Sheffield United for 32 years from 1942 to 1974.

It's very different in the modern football world. Steve Massey lasted just three days at Forfar Athletic in 1980. Although Kevin Cullis, of Swansea, lasted longer than the Forfar gaffer, his demise was probably more spectacular. Appointed on 8 February 1996, he took charge of the Swindon home game which the Swans lost 0–1. At the time, I was living in Swansea, and used to watch some of their home games. The disbelief around the city when he was appointed was palpable. His only football experience had been running an under-12s team at Cradley Town in the West Midlands (Regional) League. Cullis' only qualification for this hot seat seems to be that he was big friends with the then Swansea chairman. Three days after the Swindon defeat, the Swans were away at Blackpool. At half-time they were trailing 4–0 and, apparently, Cullis sat in the changing room with his head in his hands. He had no idea what to do. He verbally handed in his resignation and two senior players gave the team talk. The team conceded no more goals, losing 4–0. That meant that his tenure as manager lasted six days and one and a half games.

WHO WOULD IT BE?

For years in the Vanarama National League we'd been the poor relations. While teams like Salford City and Forest Green Rovers bankrolled their way into League Two of the English Football League, we stood by and smiled politely. We could only afford players no one else wanted. Or, from time to time, the local press would headline the fact that we were signing ex-Manchester United or Manchester City players, or sometimes even someone from mighty Liverpool. It was only when you read down into the body of the article that the realisation dawned on you that they'd never played for the first team. They were usually nothing more than Academy rejects.

It was a similar tale with managers. There was the odd exception, when someone who'd managed at the highest level took over. The name Brian Little readily springs to mind, but we all know how successful he was, taking us into non-league. Usually, when there was a managerial vacancy, the board would trawl the lower reaches of football. Was the top man at Llansantffraid's Total Network Solutions interested? Or how about the Connah's Quay or Brackley Town managers?

In the local bars, after the fifth or sixth pint had flowed, the Wrexham fans dreamed their dreams. Pep Guardiola or even Jürgen Klopp would be a good fit, wouldn't they? By the next morning reality had kicked in and we all avidly read the papers to see who were the favourites to be the new manger of Ryan and Rob's team.

'HE'D BE GOOD', OR 'PLEASE GOD, NO' – FANS AND BOOKIES CHOOSE THEIR MAN

While fans were having their private say about who they'd like and who they'd hate to take over, the press were busy telling readers who the bookies' favourites were. On 1 June 2021 they informed the readership that Micky Mellon had been one of their favourites, but the lure of a return to the Rovers – that's Tranmere Rovers not the Rovers Return in *Coronation Street* – was too great for him and he was now installed in charge at Prenton Park. This meant that the bookies' two favourites now for the Wrexham job were Nigel Clough and Jim Gannon.

I knew of both, but like all true fans decided to cast an eye on their footballing pedigree. I love the way us fans always behave as if we run the club. I mean, what were the chances of me being invited onto the selection panel to tell them what I thought of the front runners? I would say, as likely as the *Six O'Clock News* breaking with the story that the Pope was opening a chain of nightclubs in Rome.

NIGEL?

So Nigel, the son of Old Big 'Ead, was the bookmakers' favourite to move from Mansfield to the Racecourse. It has to be said that the son always came across as a calmer, humbler person than his father. I will never forget Brian Clough coming to the Racecourse for a third-tier match against Wrexham when he was manager of Brighton & Hove Albion in the 1973–74 season. For the match, I stood on the terraces in front of what was then the Yale Stand, now known as the Wrexham Lager Stand. I was standing near the halfway line, close to the team dugout. Instead of sitting in the dugout, Brian Clough had asked for a chair on which he sat near the touchline for the entirety of the game. This decision did not go down well with the fans, especially those of us near the front. He was blocking our view. Despite several polite and not so polite requests for him to shift and move back to the dugout, he stayed where he was. When interviewed the next day by a BBC Wales radio presenter who wanted to know why he had sat there, he came up with a priceless response: 'There were 16,000 fans here tonight. They didn't come to see Brighton or Wrexham. They came to see me.' I suppose he can be excused for his arrogance. After all, he won the first-tier championship as manager of Derby County and went on to achieve great things in the English Football League and in Europe with Nottingham Forest. During his tenure at the City Ground, he won the First Division Championship (now called the Premiership), the League Cup four times and the European Cup twice.

Of course, son Nigel was himself a great success in the world of football. As a player he scored over 100 goals in over 300 appearances for Nottingham Forest, many of them under the managership of his dad. After Forest he had spells with Liverpool, Manchester City and Sheffield Wednesday. Then, in 1998, at the age of 32, he dropped into non-league and became player-manager at Burton Albion. For a decade he was in charge at the club, and for the first five years played a major part on the field as well as off it. When appointed, Burton were in the Southern League Premier Division, the seventh tier of the Football League. Clough took them into the fifth tier, now called the Vanarama National League (but then known as the Blue Square League). In the 2008–09 season he left Burton to take over Derby County, before managing Sheffield United. In 2015 he returned to Burton where, by now, they were in League One having enjoyed their first promotion from

League Two the previous season, under the management of Jimmy Floyd Hasselbaink. In Clough's first season after his return, he guided them to runners-up spot, so they were promoted to the Championship. This meant that the incredible story of a rise from the seventh tier to the Championship was now complete. In January 2019 they reached the semi-final of the League Cup before bowing out. In May 2020 he stepped down as manger due to the financial effects of Covid-19.

So, here was a favourite, according to the bookies, who had played a major part in the rise of a club from the Southern League Premier Division to the English Football League Championship and the semi-finals of the football League Cup. Well he'll do, won't he, I thought to myself. In addition, our new chief executive, Fleur Robinson, had worked with Nigel at Burton. But, before I could throw my hat into the Clough corner, there was more homework to do. Bring on Jim Gannon.

CLOCKING JIM GANNON

If in my research Nigel Clough came across as Mr Peace and Humility, then Jim Gannon was chalk to Cloughie Junior's cheese. Loved by the fans, he was a legend at Stockport County both as a player and a manager. At County he occupied the hot seat on three separate occasions. The club obviously held him in the highest esteem. As I started to delve into his past records as a manager, a very different picture emerged. On one occasion the *Guardian* newspaper summed up his man-management skills with, 'it's either his way or the highway'. That view is certainly proved when you consider some of the scrapes he got himself into as a manager.

At Dundalk he lasted just six months, and before anyone thinks that that's not a bad stretch I need to point out that three of those were in the close season! After a longish reign of four years at Stockport he went on to manage Motherwell in Scotland. In his six months at the Fir Park stadium, he had an ongoing and acrimonious argument with the Scottish Football League. He told officials in high places that the referees in Scotland were so awful that they were bringing the game into disrepute. He publicly criticised his predecessor Mark McGhee, and fell out with club captain Stephen Craigan. Within six months of his 'leadership', the directors came to the conclusion the relationship between them and Gannon had broken down. Describing him as a 'loose Gannon' rather than a loose cannon, they eventually sacked him.

By his standards, his stint at Peterborough was successful and almost amicable. Although only in charge from February 2010 to the end of the season, he left despite being offered a new contract. He declined, saying that, with his family still living in Stockport, he needed to be closer to them. So he plumped for Port Vale, where he was confirmed as the new manager on 6 January 2011.

If Motherwell was bad, his time in charge of the Valiants must be described as disastrous – there is no other word for it. Soon after being appointed as their manager, the players at Vale Park arranged to meet the directors to share the fact that they could not get on with their new manager. Even the local daily paper, the *Sentinel*, joined in the clamour for Gannon to be relieved of the top job.

During his whole career as a manager the story that emerges is one of an individual who wants everything done his way. He's the top man at the club and, therefore, everything he says goes. Most of the clubs he managed eventually came to the conclusion that this would not work. Apart from Peterborough, where the club didn't want him to go, he seemed to do well as a manager at Stockport County. I've no doubt this was because, as a player, he was a club legend among the fans and directors. Even so, in the 2021–22 season, despite the team being high in the Vanarama National League, he was sacked by Stockport County. The directors admitted they and everyone else had had enough of his bullish leadership.

WHO DO THE FANS WANT?

After delving so deeply into the life of Gannon, I decided it was time to abandon the exercise and find out who the fans wanted. As the local daily paper reported, the fans plumped for a huge range of candidates:

Y Cae Ras, a fan who calls himself after the Welsh name of Wrexham's ground, suggested Graeme Jones. For years Jones was Roberto Martinez' number two at Swansea, Wigan and Everton. The two Colemans were popular with some fans: John of Accrington Stanley, and Chris, the ex-Wales manager, who against all odds took Wales to the semi-finals of the UEFA Euro 2016 tournament. Keith Hill of Rochdale, and Mike Flynn of Newport County, also met the approval of some fans. However, it has to be said that while they both had done well with struggling clubs, neither of them had set the world on fire in terms of promotions or silverware. Some fans touted big names, with Mark Hughes, Tony Pulis, Ian Holloway and Eddie Howe all being mentioned in the fans' dispatches. On 2 June 2021 there were some measured, interesting statements by fans reported in the *Leader* newspaper.

Sean wistfully asked, 'Can we now attract well-known names from the Football League? My hunch is that we will see an unknown who has been a successful coach elsewhere.' Matthew Sutton went down a similar track when he said, 'The club's new profile and the spotlight which will now be on it means the new incumbent needs to have a bit of ego/ personality.' Wjona Devitt hit many nails on the head when musing, 'I'd like to see a modern coaching set-up, forward thinking and using analysis and data, but also a good man-manager, as we're going to have a lot of focus on us and perhaps bigger egos than we've experienced before.'

Many fans stated that Dave Challinor, who at the end of 2020–21 won a pulsating play-off final at Ashton Gate, Bristol, to take Hartlepool back into the English Football League, was their favourite for the job. The bookmakers were in agreement with the football fans, as in early June they announced odds of 4/6 for the Chester-born manager. Despite many fans writing to the local paper and giving their allegiance to him, the man himself sounded less optimistic. While acknowledging that he was flattered to be linked with the vacancy, he explained he hadn't been contacted by anyone.

WREXHAM GET THEIR MAN

When my friend and neighbour told me in early July who the Wrexham board had appointed to manage the club, I was dumbstruck. The man they were entrusting with leading them into the golden era of Hollywood ownership was Phil Parkinson. Phil Parkinson? The manager of Altrincham? I had nothing against him personally, and whenever I'd seen him at matches or read what he'd said after games, he'd always struck me as a good and decent man. But he'd hardly set the world of football alight, had he? I mean, in all fairness, there were probably very few people in the Manchester area who'd heard of him. By now my neighbour was getting concerned and anxious about my reaction. When it was explained to me that it was not that Phil Parkinson, but the one who had taken Bradford City to the League Cup final at Wembley and won promotion for them from League One to the Championship, I was relieved. Of course, this football legend who was making his way to my favourite team's hot seat had also led Colchester United and Bolton Wanderers from League One to the Championship. As far as I was concerned, it was a great appointment and I looked forward to making the journey with him in his first season at the Racecourse. Once I'd cleared up the little problem of which Phil Parkinson it was, I was able to share intriguing news, which in the future could surely be a Trivial Pursuit or a pub quiz question, or even both. In the 2021–22 season, which football manager played against himself in the league on two occasions? Just in case you haven't been keeping up, the answer is, of course, Phil Parkinson of Altrincham versus Phil Parkinson of Wrexham. My nerves settled and my mind suitably informed, I now looked forward to the start of the 2021–22 season.

Bring it on Phil. Bring it on boys.

CHAPTER 5

SPONSORSHIP AND BEHIND THE SCENES

I SUPPOSE IT'S fairly important for management to think carefully about who they ask to sponsor the club. For all the years that Forest Green Rovers were in the National League, the home fans took a lot of stick from visiting Wrexham supporters. They wanted to know, through their chants and conversations with home fans, where the chips and burgers were. This was because the club did not sell such food as it was owned by conservationist and vegan Dale Vince.

Years ago I came across a company called Raw Flow. They were a sewerage company based in Wiltshire. Just imagine if they became the main official sponsor of a football team. During a poor performance by the team, disgruntled fans could then chant that they had shite on and off the pitch. In the National League I suppose you could say that Bromley FC are in danger of such ripostes, as they are sponsored by Westminster Waste. I wonder if chants of 'You're just a waste of space' are ever uttered by home fans, or even away fans at their Westminster Waste stadium in Hayes Lane.

In the past, Coventry City's sponsors were Ricoh, who make and sell photocopiers. If the team made a scintillating move resulting in a goal, were the players made to run off 50 or even 100 copies of the same move on the field, before they progressed with the match?

Other professional clubs could also have the mickey taken out of them about their sponsors. How did Crawley Town fans feel when People's Pension became the main sponsors? Do you have to be over 60 years old to play for the club? I just hope that Forest Green Rovers managed to prove they were not guilty of producing poor football after travelling all the way from their Innocent New Lawn stadium to play their Cumbrian rivals at Barrow's Progression Solicitors stadium.

Birmingham City play at the Trillion Trophy stadium because they are sponsored by makers of the PlayStation game of the same name. If the players and staff overwhelm Trillion, they have defeated the God of Destruction and have a chance of amassing 1,215 points, which is far more than the team's expected haul for any season in the Championship. Perhaps they should abandon football and all become PlayStation professionals.

No doubt the sponsors of Colchester United keep the players on their toes. Sponsored by JobServe Community, at least the players know that if the manager gives them the push, the sponsors should be able to help them find gainful employment pretty quickly.

There is no doubt that the emergence of Ryan and Rob as co-owners helped us massively as a club. There was no longer any need to tout the support of companies fans had never heard of, or local corner shops.

With my famous non-grasp of all things technical and computer based, when I saw that TikTok were one of Wrexham's main sponsors, I wondered if they were something to do with Swiss clockmakers. My techno savvy buddies soon put me right. I now know they host a variety of short videos, some lasting only 15 seconds, which is roughly the duration of good passages of play at the Racecourse in the past few years. In fairness, I should point out that the TikTok maximum for videos is ten minutes. Since the Hollywood takeover and the signing of new players, it would be unfair of me not to admit that some of the football I've seen at the Racecourse has been scintillating and often lasted far longer than ten minutes.

Expedia are also listed as one of Wrexham's major sponsors. The online travel company has more than 14,000 employees on their books. Their name comes from a combination of two words, speed and exploration. Since the new ownership we have seen great movement and a willingness to explore all the options by management and backroom staff.

With Ryan's Aviation American Gin also supporting the club, I wonder if in the future, instead of a break for water bottles, we might just see the players traipse to the touchline for a slug of gin.

In addition, Ifor Williams Trailers have been a faithful sponsor and supporter of the club. Williams Trailers are dear to my heart as, when I worked as a fundraiser for a homeless organisation in Cardiff, they were great supporters of those without a home or shelter.

At the time of writing, these sponsors are supporting the clubs mentioned. I realise that nowadays sponsors can change year-on-year.

TOP TEAM OFF THE PITCH TOO

While I was thrilled that Phil Parkinson, known affectionately as Parky, was on his way to manage my club, there was plenty of other news to shake me from my miserable slumbers of the past 15 years.

At the beginning of June 2021 it was announced that Les Reed, who had been the technical director for the Football Association of England, was joining the Wrexham backroom staff. Les was going to oversee which players from Dean Keates' squad should be shown the door and, along with Peter Moore of Liverpool, would make suggestions to the new manager about possible recruitments to the playing squad. Wow! But the backroom reshuffle was not over and done with yet. The previous day, Fleur Robinson had taken over as chief executive. As already noted, she had overseen the meteoric rise of Burton Albion from the seventh tier to the Championship.

Just when I thought my heart could take no more excitement or strain, I discovered that Shaun Harvey was also helping with the recruitment of new players. Shaun also took up his role as an advisor to the board. He was a key figure who helped guide Bradford City to the Premiership in 1999. After his great exploits in Yorkshire, he became the chief executive officer of the English Football League from 2013 to 2017, and now here he was at the Racecourse ready to guide Wrexham towards the heady heights of the Premiership. We hope!

CHAPTER 6

WHO'S BEEN CLIMBING THE SLAG HEAP?

MY FATHER WAS of mining stock. Before moving to Wrexham he worked in pits such as Horden colliery in County Durham and even played the euphonium for the colliery's brass band. He was a gifted musician, and a euphonium soloist at the Royal Albert Hall for the band when they won the Class Three National Competition.

In the 1930s my father and two of his older brothers, plus their father, walked from County Durham to north Wales to find work. The long walk led to them settling in the Wrexham area. They initially opened their own open-cast mine on Ponciau Banks in Rhosllanerchrugog. Sadly, it proved to be non-viable and the male members of the family all went to work in one or other of the coal mines that dotted the north-east Wales landscape in those days. My father had five brothers and two sisters, all of whom settled in the Wrexham area eventually.

I was very aware from an early age of the dangerous job my father did. When I was four he had a horrendous accident at Bersham colliery when the roof fell in on top of him. The 'powers that be' gave him no compensation because they claimed the props holding up the roof had not been properly secured. As a child and an adult, I have often imagined what it must have been like in those dark underground lanes they walked, getting to places to use their picks to hack away at coal seams. For eight hours every day he was in another world, where the sun had no chance of shining. He was tall, six foot two inches in height, and once told me that every day when the cage carrying the miners reached the bottom, he had to walk underground from Bersham to Coedpoeth, a good couple of miles, before he began his shift. At one point the roof above him was just three foot six inches high. At several stages he would have to crawl. When I was older I was so relieved when he told me I could pursue any occupation, except being a coal miner. He expressed similar views to my brothers Phil and Jim.

My father lost his younger brother Lloyd in the Gresford disaster of 22 September 1934 when 266 miners were killed in what turned out to be the worst pit explosion ever in north Wales, and the fourth worst in Wales. For those and many other reasons I find it difficult to romanticise about pits and slag heaps. So I was amazed when, in the late 1990s, a huge sign was erected on Bersham slag heap. Some young men had braved methane underfoot and several other potential pitfalls to clamber up to the top and unfurl a banner saying HOLLYWOOD. Aled Lewis Evans is a well-known poet, who was born in Barmouth but has lived for many years in Wrexham where his family moved to when Aled's father became postmaster of Town Hill Post Office. In one of his poems Aled tells the story:

A Hollywood sign was temporarily erected on Bersham Pit Head

'They've pulled it down.'
I had been searching,
had dragged my father to see
the Hollywood sign in Rhostyllen.

'I've heard someone say there's a sign up, like in Los Angeles.'
My father, gobsmacked, muttered,

'The only place I know of in Rhostyllen
where there's a hill of any kind
is the old slag heap by the Little Chef.'

For a short period only
the old Bersham Pit Head
had presented celluloid dreams,
a multicoloured vision
in magic letters – HOLLYWOOD.
Sparkling dreams were scattered
on old redundant slag heaps.

'They've taken it down mate.'
Someone had had their
fifteen minutes of fame.

An April Fool prank
by lads from Chirk.
It was announced that such letters would distract
travellers on the bypass
and the letters would be dragged away.

Dreams no longer remained on the hillside.

We in borderland scramble once more for a dream.
This one ended in the locked shafts of mediocrity.
Forgotten like a quick joyride down the bypass.

But it did happen.
Inspiring each of us
to strive for the Yellow Brick Road,
that thread of gold beyond the bypass.

(Adapted from the Welsh by Aled Lewis Evans)

So it was a surprise to us older inhabitants of the town
to see the prank being re-enacted in August 2021. A huge
sign saying WREXHAM appeared on top of Bersham slag
heap. All kinds of conjecture floated around the town. Most

people's favourite assumption, one week ahead of the start of the 2021–22 season, was that Ryan and Rob were behind the prank. The rumour was they'd probably paid someone to do it for them. Articles in the *Daily Post*, *The Leader*, *North Wales Live* on the web, plus items on BBC news meant more publicity and fuelled the guessing game even further. However, Ryan and Rob were quick to distance themselves from the sign, and slowly but surely people began to believe them.

The *Deadpool* star poured cold water on the view that he had done it, but said he'd wished he'd come up with the idea on Twitter: 'I wish I'd thought of that. But if I were to really dig into it, I wish I wasn't someone who wished they'd thought of it.' Some newspapers hailed the appearance of the sign as a 'sensation'.

As already noted, this was not the first time that someone had put a statement on top of the tip. Interestingly, the Hollywood sign of the Nineties achieved a lot more than inspiring Aled the poet to write his poem. It had also caused a furore, and I believe the two youngsters responsible were fined for their troubles.

In the early Noughties a sign saying 'Hamilton Out' also appeared on Bersham slag heap. This appeared during the fans' successful High Court fight to stop Hamilton in his battle for ownership of the Racecourse Ground. A judge ruled that the valuable freehold of Wrexham Football Club's ground was 'vested in the club' not in Hamilton.

In 2016 a three-and-a-half metre sculpture was secretly erected on the slag heap, an art exhibition by Wrexham artist and painter Ian Walton. With help from many local inhabitants, he erected it as a monument to the town's industrial heritage. Built from 70 metres of steel, the art work consisted of 120 kilograms of concrete to keep it in place and the whole structure was paid for by the artist.

The riddle of who put WREXHAM on top of the slag heap

persisted right up to the start of the football season. On the day that the 2020–21 season started, the papers revealed that the sign had been put there by Vanarama who were the main sponsors of the National League. The stunt was carried out to draw attention to themselves and the league.

The owners of the site, Bersham (Glenside) Limited, eventually ordered that the sign be taken down. So no more parked cars were to be seen on the road at the side of the old Bersham colliery, and no more brave tourists clambering up the slag heap to take photographs of the sign. There were also no more sweeping claims that the WREXHAM sign on the slag heap would rival the Angel of the North sculpture. It meant that, at long last, we could get on with the football season.

CHAPTER 7

BRING ON THE FOOTY

FOLLOWING WREXHAM IS never ever straightforward, and that was proved at the beginning of the new season. When the referee's whistle heralded the start of the 2021–22 season for Wrexham at Solihull Moors, it was the end of a long break from football for Wrexham fans. However, Phil Parkinson and his management team had been anything but inactive. The following ten players had been snapped up by the Reds: Shaun Brisley, Aaron Hayden, Jake Hyde, Paul Mullin, Harry Lennon, David Jones, Bryce Hosannah, James Jones, Ben Tozer, Liam McAlinden. Four of the new signings made the starting line-up, while two ended up on the bench. All the signings were impressive and all of them were from EFL clubs. There was no doubt, looking at the boys donning Wrexham's red for the first time, that Parkinson had got some class players to sign for the club. The three standouts for me were Mullin, Tozer (not playing at Solihull) and Hayden.

One thousand fans made the journey from north Wales and were nearly half the official attendance of 2,196. This turned out to be an indication of the away support Wrexham would get for the rest of the season. Of course, Wrexham were not supposed to be playing at Solihull in the season's opening game. The scheduled match was to be at home, against Yeovil, but the Somerset club had to cancel due to Covid. Solihull were due to play Dover, but the Kent side also cancelled. Please don't get me going about Dover! They spent the previous season cancelling all their games. Despite that, instead of being thrown out of the league they were allowed to take their place for the 2021–22 season with a 12-point deduction. They showed their appreciation to the powers-that-be by cancelling their opener.

From Wrexham's point of view, the Solihull match got off to a wobbly start. Goalkeeper Christian Dibble allowed the ball to go through his legs. It seemed as if we were going to concede a bizarre opening goal, before Hayden stepped in and cleared. Later in the half Solihull went ahead. In the second half Wrexham edged in front with goals by Mullin and a 'worldie' by Dave Jones. So the Wrexham fans were now in fine voice as we headed towards the final whistle. Two of the new signings had scored for us on the opening day of the season. It was a good omen. But this was Wrexham. Right at the death, Solihull Moors equalised with just two minutes to go.

There is an extraordinary fact about the results on that opening day of the Vanarama National League: Aldershot 0 Chesterfield 2; Barnet 0 Notts County 5; Halifax 1 Maidenhead 2; Kings Lynn Town 0 Southend United 1; Stockport County 1 Dagenham & Redbridge 3; Torquay United 1 Altrincham 3; Wealdstone 1 Woking 2; Weymouth 0 Boreham Wood 2; Solihull Moors 2 Wrexham 2.

In nine matches played, not one of the teams playing at home won. The other chilling fact for me, as a fan, was that the only team playing away that failed to win was, of course, my beloved Wrexham!

The first home game in Rob and Ryan's first full season in charge was to Notts County who, along with Wrexham, were one of the favourites to do well that year. In the lead-up to the game, I realised that I was in a spot of bother. Here I was, commissioned by a publisher to put my impressions of the season into print, but struggling to get a ticket. The capacity for the game had been dropped to 5,500 because the WREXRENT Stand was not yet ready.

Only people with season tickets were able to see the match. Anxious to see all the home games, I had applied for a press pass but, despite enlisting the help of prominent people at the club, I was unable to get even a response. A 'no' would have been more pleasing than a blank silence. The game was just a few days away and I was heading towards streaming or listening on the radio. Tracy, my hairdresser, asked if I was going to the match. I explained my dilemma. Her son Louis had a season ticket but wouldn't be going as his wife was expecting a baby any day. Thank God for the wonder of birth, I say. So I paid for the equivalent of a match-day ticket and left the hairdresser's salon with a stylish haircut and a promised ticket for the big match.

WREXHAM V NOTTS COUNTY

Although disappointed that the ground was only going to be half full, there was still a wonderful buzz of anticipation in the air as I made my 20-minute walk to the ground from my house. The night was as cold as the inside of a freezer. Having been told by doctors (more of that later) that I could still watch football as long as I dressed up warmly, I was spectacularly overdressed: two pairs of socks, a thermal vest bought from a mountain climbing shop, a thick shirt, two pullovers, Wrexham scarf tied around my neck tightly, black leather gloves and a pom-pom hat that announced Wrexham's Red Army was on its way. I probably looked like an actor auditioning for a part as Billy Bunter attempting to ascend the Eiger.

Once on Regent Street, which leads into Mold Road where the ground is situated, I started to encounter Wrexham fans. Ahead of me were young boys and girls donning shirts advertising Ryan Reynolds' Aviation American Gin. Were they old enough to wear those shirts or should they be 18? For years, successive managers claimed they wanted to make the Racecourse a fortress. Now, with the sponsorship of an alcoholic drink, I asked myself whether there was any danger of the ground becoming a gin palace. As well as lots of children, I realised there were far more women heading for the stadium than I ever saw in the games before lockdown. No doubt this was the Rob and Ryan effect. Also, for days before the game, rumours had floated around that the duo were going to turn up for the match.

It was a pulsating game and, despite the fact that Notts County went ahead in the first half, Paul Mullin got his first Racecourse goal for the club in the second half to give us a 1–1 draw. That meant that in our opening three games we'd won one (away to Eastleigh) and drawn two. That gave us a return of five points from three games. Many fans were already muttering but I consoled myself that there was still a lot of season to go. After watching the Notts County performance, I realised it had been a long time since I had seen so much running off the ball by men in Wrexham shirts. We had looked good against an excellent team.

BIG SEPTEMBER CROWDS AND STILL HUNTING TICKETS

Back in August I'd walked to the ticket office to try and buy a ticket for the Notts County game. It was then that I was told that it was season ticket holders only because of the problems with the WREXRENT Stand. So I decided to go back home and see if my partner Rona would like a ticket for next Saturday's game at home against Woking. It was back to the Racecourse for my solitary ticket. 'Sorry,' said the girl, 'I can't sell you one, I'm sorry.' They were only selling tickets a week before the match, and first chance of purchase would go to members. Despite being a member, this meant I couldn't get a ticket until the week beginning 4 September when I would be away on holiday.

Wrexham played five league games in September, and by

the end of the month their record for the new season wasn't terribly flattering. In total in the league they had played eight games, won three, drawn three and lost two, which meant that out of a possible 24 points they had bagged just 12. Already some Wrexham fans were banging the doom and woe drums.

By the end of December, which in everyone's mind represents the halfway stage of the season, there was a spectacular difference between our home form and our performances on the road. Away from the Racecourse, in 12 games we had scored 29 goals and conceded 15. At home, in nine encounters we managed just four wins, three of which were 1–0 victories and scored a paltry seven. Just in case you think we may have banged-in loads of goals in the other win, I must disappoint you. That was a 2–0 success over Bromley, who had a man sent off early in the game. This meant that, in stark contrast to our performances at other grounds, on the Racecourse pitch we managed to score just seven times between August and December in the league, and conceded five. After those statistics perhaps it was little wonder that Wrexham had such a huge following on the road. The two highlights were 1,700 fans at Stockport and 2,000 fans at Notts County.

The two home victories in September were 1–0 wins over Woking and Dagenham & Redbridge. A worrying pattern seemed to be emerging, with the home team dominating the first half, then appearing to hang on for dear life towards the end of the second half. Having said that, I still saw enough in those games to feel that we should do well.

Sat in the front row of the lower Wrexham Lager Stand and very close to the dugout, I imagined Phil Parkinson a calm, quiet, very together kind of person. But I ended up with a very different impression. He is often cautioned by the ref and, I have to admit, I love his passion and involvement in the game.

STILL IN THE CUP, THE RAINS COME DOWN AND STARS COME TO TOWN

October didn't start too well for Wrexham. On the first Saturday of the month (2 October) the team and about 800 Wrexham fans made their way to Aldershot's Recreation Ground in Hampshire. For days the rain had been almost biblical in north Wales. By half-time, there were several large patches of water on the pitch in Aldershot. The referee took the players off and, although it was not certain, it seemed pretty obvious that the match would be abandoned. When the players left the pitch Wrexham were leading 0–2. Needless to say, they wanted the game to continue, whereas Aldershot wanted it to be called off. Cue some of the Wrexham players coming on to the pitch with brushes to try and get rid of the surface water. The referee then announced he would check it later, after which he would give his final decision. Those Wrexham players who had come back to try and rescue the game were playing a blinder with their brushes. Barry Horne, who was the summariser on Radio Wales, had already jumped into his car and was heading back to north Wales, assuming the match was off. However, the radio powers-that-be phoned him on his mobile and told him to return to the ground as the game might still be on. Eventually, the referee re-emerged to inspect the pitch. He walked into the sheeting rain, just as Barry Horne rolled up in his car for the restart! As expected, the game was called off. It was a great shame as Wrexham were leading at a ground that is rarely a happy hunting place for them.

October didn't start well for me, either. In September 2018 I was rushed to hospital with chest pains and severe breathing difficulties. After extensive tests over a period of months, it was discovered that both the right and left ventricles in the heart were failing. Only functioning at 37 per cent capacity, it meant that many of the things I'd been able to do in the past I now struggled with. Looked after brilliantly by the heart team, I was told that mine was a hidden disease. The medics also shared the joyous news that I would probably last between five and ten years. Being an optimist, I think I'll plump for the ten-year prediction. Besides, I've met someone with the same problem who has exceeded the final prediction by three years and is still going strong. Suffering as I do with this condition, I've realised how easy it is to let illness define me. Instead, I concentrate on all the wonderful friends I still have and all the enjoyable things I can still do – such as following Wrexham with two Hollywood co-owners at the helm. It keeps me going and keeps me smiling.

The uncertainty whether I would be fit enough to watch all the home matches was one of the reasons I decided against trying for a season ticket. The other factor was that, as a full-time writer and performer, I sometimes got bookings for Saturday events. I watch Wrexham at home mainly, as many of the grounds in the Vanarama National League only have standing areas for away fans. Being on my feet for a long time is something I can no longer do. My condition is also the reason why I missed the Chesterfield match at home on Tuesday, 5 October. The day before, I was taken into A&E at Wrexham hospital with a recurrence of my problem and difficulty in breathing. For three hours I sat in an ambulance waiting outside the hospital. The paramedic was a fascinating person, and we chatted about anything and everything while he monitored my heart. He told me that he had gone to school at Ysgol Llangefni in Sir Fôn (Anglesey). Bizarrely, I did my teaching practice there when I was a student at Bangor University. Checking dates, we discovered that I had taught him briefly. He was far too polite to add 'not very well'.

It was tempting for me to think that once they'd wheeled me into hospital that I'd be seen straightaway. No chance. I sat in a wheelchair for 15 hours before I was seen. I was waiting throughout the night. As there was no heating on, it felt as cold, if not colder inside as it had been outside. I was eventually checked out and sent home in the afternoon.

Which is why I missed the Chesterfield match. Not having slept for over 24 hours, I was absolutely exhausted. I caught snatches of the match as I dozed in and out of consciousness. Quite frankly, I'm pleased I missed the game. It sounded as bad as the weather, and ended in a 1–1 draw with Paul Mullin snatching an equaliser at the death. A staggering 9,147 watched the game. If it hadn't been for my medical blip, I could have carried the attendance up to 9,148.

ON THE FA CUP TRAIL

The following Saturday was FA Cup day. We were drawn away to Marine who play in the eighth tier of English football. There were several reasons why we Wrexham fans were nervous. Although we have a great and proud history of giant-killing, both in Europe and in the FA and League Cups, we also have a less salubrious record of losing to teams who are lower than us in the league pyramid. I remember, as a Football League outfit, us getting knocked out of the FA Cup by non-league Runcorn, and later in our history losing to Worcester City. In the 2020–21 season Marine had been the giant-killers of the Cup before succumbing to Tottenham Hotspur at home, 0–5. The Marine manager was Steve Burr, who in our 15-year reign in the Vanarama National League was the only Chester manager to oversee a Cestrian victory at the Racecourse in the local derby.

Hundreds of Wrexham fans made their way to the neat little ground in Crosby on Merseyside, swelling the attendance to 1,941 in a ground that holds 2,500. For me, one of the most interesting aspects of the Crosby stadium is the grand houses which border one of the touchlines and overlook the pitch. For their third round encounter against Spurs in the previous season, I remember being impressed by the number of Crosby house owners who'd erected platforms in their gardens so that they could watch the football over the wooden fences. I had also been fascinated by the fact that their back gates had the house number painted onto them. This was so that if the ball went over one of the fences into someone's back garden, if no one was there to throw the ball back onto the pitch, one of the spectators in the ground could walk out of the ground to the front of the houses, knock on the relevant numbered house, and ask for the ball back!

In terms of the match, it was notable for a bad injury sustained by goalkeeper Rob Lainton who was carried off and replaced by substitute keeper Christian Dibble. As we headed for added time, Wrexham were losing 1–0 and heading for a Cup shock. Then, local hero Jordan Davies stepped up to score a great goal and earn a replay.

We were unable to host the replay as the pitch was being dug up and resurfaced. A great time to do it. But needs must! We made a better job of dispatching Marine and won 2–0 at Nantwich Town's ground, with Paul Mullin scoring twice.

TWO MORE FANS FOR THE GAME

Of course, the month of October will be remembered for the fact that Ryan and Rob managed to make their first appearances at two Wrexham matches. I doubt if there could have been as much anticipation or excitement for a royal visit. Following an encouraging 0–3 victory away to Barnet, the Wrexham bandwagon rolled into Maidenhead. The Maidenhead staff had kept the secret for three weeks that the Hollywood stars would be in the crowd. Wrexham fans who had made the long journey down to Berkshire, and the faithful belonging to the home team, had a great surprise and some of them were able to pose for selfies with the megastars. The other unexpected incident in the game was that the referee sent the wrong man off. The official gave Bryce Hosannah his marching orders for a foul committed by his team-mate Paul Mullin.

After that Tuesday night game, the town of Wrexham

became seriously star-struck. Even inhabitants who never read newspapers, visited social media, or listened to or watched the news must have realised something was afoot. For starters, there seemed to be almost as many workmen in orange Wrexham County Borough Council jackets around as natives of the town. We were getting ready for a VIP visit. It suddenly seemed as if very few people in Wrexham were working. They were all on the streets hoping for a glimpse of football royalty. It was rumoured that King Rob and King Ryan were going to be at the match the following Saturday when the Reds would take on Torquay United. From Wednesday to the weekend, I have never lived in such a clean, pristine town. I have never seen so many brushes in action at the same time. Watching them doing their work, swooshing and sweeping rubbish out of sight, was like watching a brush orchestra in full swing. By the time they'd finished everywhere was so clean and tidy you could have eaten your sandwiches off the streets!

ROB AND RYAN
IN TOWN FOR THE FIRST TIME

The boys met invited people for drinks at the Turf, the pub near the Racecourse Ground, a favourite haunt of many a die-hard fan. Ryan and Rob paid for all the drinks and this is just another example of the fabulous way they related to the fans from day one. I'd be hard-pressed to think of any previous owners who had been so generous and warm to fans of the club.

It's important to remember that, as noted, by this stage of their tenure the Hollywood owners had already given £6,000 to a disabled follower of Wrexham to pay for renovations to make it easier for his mobility through doorways. In the early days they also sent free bottles of Ryan's Aviation American Gin for the enjoyment of many fans.

It was no surprise that their anticipated presence at the ground saw the attendance swell, with 9,813 turning out for the match against Torquay United. As I walked to the ground I could see more youngsters and young women heading for the turnstiles. Although many had caught a glimpse of them the previous Thursday, when the stars did a walkabout on the streets of Wrexham, people just couldn't get enough of them.

Before kick-off they stood on the pitch and welcomed the massive crowd in Welsh. Sadly, the game failed to live up to expectations. By this stage of the season our four home league games had resulted in Wrexham scoring a total of just four goals in two wins and two draws. While we were on top leading 1–0 in the latter stages of this game, it has to be said that this was not one of our better performances. We were also without Paul Mullin, our star striker with ten goals at that stage of the season. This was because the FA had righted the referee's wrong decision from the Maidenhead game and banned him for three games because of the red card. In the dying moments of the game, the inevitable happened, and Torquay snatched an equaliser to head back to the West Country with a point. This meant that, for a while to come, Ryan would have to be content to follow the Reds online. This was something he did every Saturday morning with his family, at 9am American East Coast time.

PLEASE CAN WE PLAY ALL OUR GAMES AWAY FROM HOME?

At the beginning of November we lost in the FA Cup, away to Harrogate, a team who had done what we were struggling to do, climb out of the Vanarama National League and establish themselves in League Two of the English Football League. While home goals were as difficult to obtain as invitations to Buckingham Palace, we were rampant on the road. Early signs of what was to come were at the Hive in late October when we put three past Barnet in a 0–3 victory. We finally got to play 90 minutes at the Recreation Ground against Aldershot, and ran out 0–5 winners without the aid of buckets or mops! This was followed by us hitting Kings Lynn for six, with the home team only registering two. After that visit to Norfolk we beat Halifax, also pressing for a play-off spot, at the Shay, 1–2. This meant that in those three away games we'd collected nine points, scored 13 and conceded just three.

That last statistic begged the question: why were we so brilliant away and so scared of scoring goals at home in front of bumper crowds? Were the bumper crowds the problem? There were still a good half-dozen or so players in Phil Parkinson's team who had also been in Dean Keates' squad the previous season. After all, they'd have got used to playing in front of empty stadia during lockdown. Even if they remembered pre-Covid gates, they would sometimes have been performing in front of no more than 3,000. Or was the problem also with the new players? Ten of the squad had signed in the pre-season. Was it just a case of the new boys not quite gelling yet?

Whatever the reason, the home trend seemed to continue into late November and early December. Despite less than convincing performances at home, we finished the year in fifth position, nicely situated to challenge for a play-off place or even top spot and automatic promotion. At the two last home games in November, ten-man Bromley were dispatched 2–0, and in the next game, against Yeovil, it was our turn to be reduced to ten men early on when McAlinden was sent off and we lost 0–2.

THE CRUEL WINDS DO BLOW

There were all kinds of problems trying to watch football in late November and December, stretching on into early January

2022. Winds wailed around my house for several nights. On many mornings my first thought was to see whether the shed roof was still intact.

The winds which played with our emotions and our roof for several weeks also affected many games in the National League, with several postponements. For those games that went ahead, it was an ordeal for spectators watching matches in storm conditions and, of course, for the players. Clever chips by gifted players, or free kicks, were prone to move forward in the selected direction, then bend backwards and return to sender, or even leave players looking confused and stupid as the ball did more than just return, before whizzing past them.

Bizarrely, the Met Office decided to give names to these storms of the sky, which had not only caused difficulties for players but also for fans. Having been told by medics I should not venture out in adverse weather conditions, I was constantly faced with the dilemma of should I stay or should I go to a game? It's a great song but not an enjoyable state of mind.

Friends would positively say to me, 'Just wrap-up warm. You'll be fine.' Great advice but, with all the neuroses I have introduced to my health problem, wrapping up warm can take as long as the first half of a match. Layer after potential layer is examined, then discarded for another layer. Once I'm convinced I'm ready for the expedition to climb the North Face of the steps up to my seat in the upper Wrexham Lager Stand, there is always the danger I'll struggle to get through my front door. And so it goes on and on... Thank you storms Arwen, Barra, Malik, Corrie and Eunice for playing havoc with my nerves and my sleep patterns, as I often imagined my substantial shed roof floating over the wall into a garden in the street behind.

THE PROBLEM WITH
MR DRAKEFORD'S RULING

Living as I do just four miles from the English border has its advantages. But there are also difficulties with my location. These became evident to me during the Covid lockdowns. At Whitehall, Boris Johnson would announce the things we could do and couldn't do, plus where we could go and where we couldn't go. Our leader in Cardiff would wait for a week or so and then give us Welsh folk a different collection of 'dos and don'ts'. This had huge repercussions for us football fans. It meant that Wrexham could not play in front of crowds at home. This led to lots of rearranged fixtures, with us only playing in front of crowds at away venues. These rearrangements led to the bizarre situation that, after our away fixture at Chesterfield on 22 February 2022, of our next 11 league games up to 18 April (Bank Holiday Monday) against Altrincham, ten of them were at home.

DECEMBER MISSING

After 838 supporters watched the boys snatch an unconvincing win against bottom club Dover, with a late winner from Jordan Davies, next up were Weymouth at the Racecourse. The TV cameras were due in town to cover this one live on 11 December, the day before my birthday. Thank goodness for that timing. I'd be able to enjoy some food and vat-fuls of alcohol with water as a side dish. This would give me several hours to recover before taking my seat in the Wrexham Lager Stand.

However, dreadful news was broken to me which explains why there had been a few hushed telephone conversations by my partner in the past few weeks leading up to my birthday. Daughters, grandchildren and my brother and his wife were making their way to Wrexham for a pre-booked meal at the wonderful Cross Foxes restaurant in Erbistock for six o'clock, just 40 minutes after kick-off. There were just a few days for me to build up my diminishing stocks of gracious joy about this unexpected meal.

Once I'd got over the trauma that they all had something else to do on my actual birthday, my excitement grew at the fact that I would be seeing all my offspring. It was important that no one brought a smart phone or something else to the restaurant to take a sneaky view of what was going on at the Racecourse. When I heard details of the missed game, I was relieved I'd not seen the drab 1–0 win for Wrexham. Despite the three points, friends told me that I'd missed nothing and certainly media reports proved that my mates were not just being kind. There is something about Wrexham Football Club and live TV coverage. They haven't always mixed very well.

Many fans must have realised this fact before kick-off. We had all been getting used to crowds at home of well over 8,000. Whether it was that this fixture was too close to Christmas, or the fact that it was viewable on BT Sport, I will never know. Whatever the reason, we had our lowest league attendance of 7,530. For all the walking encyclopaedias reading this, and I know there are a huge number of you out there, I'm sure a good many of you are screaming 'Notts County'. As already mentioned, the attendance that night was only 5,456 due to the fact that the WREXRENT Stand was closed.

After the Weymouth victory, we beat Gloucester City 5–0 at home in the Buildbase FA Trophy. What was impressive about Gloucester was that they refused to cancel the match, despite having an outbreak of Covid which affected many of their first-choice squad. Instead, they went ahead with the fixture and fielded a youthful side. We then ended the month with a 0–2 away win at Altrincham where Phil Parkinson pitted his wits against Phil Parkinson.

The new year started for us at Notts County. Reece Hall-Johnson scored in the opening minutes. However, a few minutes later, with goalkeeper Lainton beaten, Harry Lennon handled on the line. The penalty was easily scored and we went on to lose 3–1.

Folkestone Invicta were next up in the FA Trophy. Mercifully, we were victorious against Invicta with no banana skins in sight. Back in the league, a tough tussle ensued against ex-Wrexham hero Shaun Pearson and his new club Grimsby. During that day, 25 January, Wrexham made the kind of signing that could only be made by a National League club with the backing of Hollywood millionaires. Ollie Palmer, a striker from League One side Wimbledon, signed on the dotted line for a mouth-watering fee of £300,000. Just 90 minutes before kick-off, our new striker was introduced to his team-mates. Phil Parkinson obviously took the view that the best place to meet your new work colleagues was on the pitch. He was announced as number 35 on the Tannoy to tumultuous applause and deafening cheers by the majority of the 8,434 crowd. We won by a 1–0 scoreline. Who scored the winner? New boy Ollie, of course. Since Jake Hyde's injury early in the season and his long absence, it was obvious that our prolific marksman Paul Mullin was missing someone who could play alongside him and create a dual strike force. Those 90 minutes suggested Wrexham had found that player in Ollie Palmer.

ARE WE GOING TO WIN THE CHAMPIONSHIP?

At the beginning of April, Wrexham were 11 points adrift of runaway leaders Stockport. By the time we played them in our final home match of the season, we were just three points behind them. Not even the most ardent home fans were getting too carried away before kick-off, though.

County had sold 1,214 tickets to their fans and the far end of the Wrexham Lager Stand was packed to the rafters with the County faithful. They were in fine voice as they knew what three points for their team meant. A Stockport victory would see the Hatters head back to Cheshire as champions of the Vanarama National League. Inevitably, there were one or two disgruntled home fans who, when Wrexham were looking to replace their sacked manager Dean Keates, had wanted Dave Challinor as Wrexham's manager. When it came to managing teams, he certainly seemed to have the golden Midas touch. He had already won championships with Colwyn Bay, Stockport, Fylde and Hartlepool and was now on the brink of taking his beloved team Stockport back into the Football League.

ME AND THE MISSING GAME SYNDROME

There is something about me and vital games. For whatever reason, I inevitably seem to miss them. When I started watching Wrexham as a child, in their promotion-winning season of 1962, I saw them at the majority of their home games. One I missed was at home to Hartlepool United. The weather was bad, and for some reason Mr Gibson was unable to take me. So instead I went to watch my local team, Rhos Aelwyd, of the division one Wrexham area Welsh National League, play at Ponciau Banks. As often happened at that level of football, certain members of the crowd had transistor radios with them. It was often the case that the match they were watching was so bad that it was better to be tuned into another one. Even though they could only hear rather than see it, they spent 90 minutes building my sense of gloom that I was at the wrong venue. The transistor fans kept shouting out the score when a goal went in at the Racecourse. And I can tell you, there were plenty of them. Eleven in all. Mercifully, ten went to Wrexham, with the north-east team getting a consolation goal to take back on what must have been a fairly miserable journey on the team coach. Wrexham's highest score in the league ever, 10–1, a record that still stands to this day. And I wasn't there.

On the Thursday, just a few days before the Sunday, 8 May, kick-off against Stockport County, I was very poorly most of the night. Smitten with a recurrence of the heart condition, I hardly slept and was in a lot of pain. I was determined not to call an ambulance. With the difficulties facing the National Health Service, I knew that I would be waiting for hours. As mentioned, the last time I'd been rushed in there it had been 15 hours before I was seen.

Having had this condition for four years, I was now beginning to learn that these bouts left me feeling weak and wiped out for three or four days. It was a no-brainer decision for me. I would rest and, on the third day, aptly a Sunday, I would rise from the bed, rather than the dead. To save walking, Rona would drive me to the ground, then pick me up after the final whistle.

Sadly it was not to be. The Hartlepool syndrome kicked in. From early on Sunday, I knew there was no chance of me making the Stockport County match either by foot or by car. There was nothing I could do except resign myself to bed and Radio Wales. Rona had my ticket and she saw a game that encouraged adjectives such as 'superlative', 'brilliant' and 'unbelievable' from all those who watched Wrexham demolish Stockport by three goals to nil. To rub salt into their wounds, we leapfrogged County to the top of the table. Despite having the same number of points, with 91 goals scored and only 43 conceded, we had a better goal difference. This meant that we were champions-elect by the skin of our teeth.

The rest of Sunday and all day Monday were glorious days for us Wrexham fans. We strutted around the place and told anyone who would listen or read our messages on social media that we were top of the table, heading for the English Football League. On Tuesday, we briefly abandoned shouting for and singing the praises of Wrexham, and became Torquay United fans. Torquay were due at Edgeley Park to play Stockport that evening. It was a game in hand for both teams. Although in mid-table, under Gary Johnson, Torquay had made a late climb up the table and, at one stage, looked as though they might make it to the play-offs. In addition, the Gulls had beaten both Stockport and Notts County at their own grounds earlier in the season. They had also spoiled the party for Rob McElhenney and Ryan Reynolds when they had arrived at the Racecourse in late October to watch the Wrexham v Torquay fixture. Although we led for most of the game, the away team had pulled one back in the dying moments and snatched a 1–1 draw. With this good track record against the two top teams I, along with thousands of other Wrexham fans, was hopeful they would do us all a favour and go back to the south-west with three points in their pockets.

As I had 'previous' with the Church, I wondered whether prayers of intercession for one's favourite football team were permissible up above. The more I thought about it, the more uncertain I became about the ethics of such a gamble. What I was doing was asking the Almighty to be Torquay's 12th man, and score a goal for them on Wrexham's behalf. Where did that put Stockport if they were praying for a victory over Torquay. And perhaps, much more importantly, what about God himself? Wouldn't this proposed transaction of mine put the deity in a right pickle?

Faced with all these imponderables, I decided to let the game run its own course. When the referee blew the final whistle it signalled a 1–0 win for the Hatters, and Stockport were once again three points clear at the top going into the last game. Perhaps I should have prayed after all. It now meant that we had to win our last game and get the prayer mats out for Halifax to beat Stockport at Edgeley Park.

HERE WE GO AGAIN

Soccer pundits always say it's tight at the top but, while it's in danger of being a tired cliché, it was certainly the case in the Vanarama National League on 15 May 2022, the last day of the season. Wrexham or Stockport could finish the day as champions, and if Chesterfield lost and Dagenham & Redbridge won, they would knock Chesterfield out of the last play-off place. Just over 1,000 fans made the arduous journey from north Wales to Essex. It meant that a third of the 3,470 crowd were following the away team. For a good hour before kick-off they were in tremendous voice, singing their songs and chanting the names of their heroes. After 90 minutes in which Wrexham barely got going, they would have been forgiven if they had been totally silent after Dagenham won 3–0. But they weren't. Instead, they gave voice to their pride in the way Wrexham had played throughout the season – in finishing second. It was all to play for in the semi-final of the play-offs against either Notts County or Grimsby, plus the Buildbase FA Trophy final at Wembley the following Sunday against Bromley.

WEMBLEY FINAL

Having watched Wrexham since the 1961–62 season, I had to wait until 2005 before I could watch my team in a Wembley trophy final. Wrexham got there after a thrilling semi-final victory against Oldham Athletic over two legs, a 3–5 win away and 1–0 at the Racecourse. This meant that we were through to the LDV Vans Trophy final in April 2005. During its history this tournament has enjoyed, or perhaps endured, several name changes. Many refer to it by its unsponsored name and still call it the Football League Trophy. I had tickets for my brother and myself, but neither of us were to see our dream of watching the team we'd followed since childhood play at Wembley. The great stadium was being rebuilt, so the game was rescheduled for the Millennium Stadium in Cardiff. We left early in the morning and drove to Cardiff. One Wrexham fan described this route as an epic journey past milk churns and through the farmyards of Shropshire and Herefordshire. Despite the challenges of the trip, it was hugely enjoyable. We were in a massive convoy of cars and coaches, all making their way to the Welsh capital to cheer on the boys to a 2–0 victory over Southend United. The irony of that game and result was the fact that we were a League One side and Southend were in League Two. By the time the next season started, Southend were in League One and we were a League Two outfit on the slippery slope to the obscurity of non-league football.

In view of this, I suppose we're not allowed to call this a Wembley appearance, although it should have been. Our first actual appearance at Wembley was in 2013, when we beat Grimsby on penalties in the FA Trophy. We were there a month later in the National League play-off which we lost to our great Welsh rivals, Newport County. In 2015, again in the FA Trophy final, we managed to throw away a 2–0 lead against North Ferriby and go 2–3 down to the village team from Yorkshire, before snatching an equaliser, and then losing 4–5 on penalties.

So, as the town of Wrexham prepared for our fourth appearance at Wembley, we went there with a record of played three, won one, lost two. Although, I'm still tempted to sneak in the Southend victory and level the score at 2–2. But I know it's not allowed.

Despite the poor performance against Dagenham & Redbridge on the last day of the season, there was still great optimism and belief among the Wrexham faithful. After all, we could all point to the fact that since the New Year the team had served up some brilliant football. Yes, Bromley were a difficult side to beat, and they had a habit of knocking out our goalkeeper. In the last two matches against them, at their ground, our keeper Rob Lainton had been carried off with serious injuries.

For a few weeks fans had confidently evoked the feat of York City who, some years previously, had managed to lift the FA Trophy and win promotion to the Football League in the same season. That prediction and nod to past history had worked for us, before we finished second. It was difficult to justify the two-pronged prediction when one of the prongs had fallen off quite spectacularly at Dagenham.

SUNDAY, 22 MAY 2022

I was determined to get down to Wembley to see this game. Every Monday I run a class for wannabe writers in Mold, nine miles from Wrexham. Having missed a few sessions due to catching Covid, I felt unable to cancel the class yet again. When I started to look at the logistics, all kinds of things transpired to pour cold water on my plans. Since hitting old age, my hobbies outside of watching football include collecting illnesses. In addition to the heart problem, I also have degenerative osteoarthritis in both knees, plus coeliac disease, which when it strikes can give me several unscheduled visits to the loo. Stuck in a bus, unable to move around, was not the recipe for an easy ride. Sunday trains running on time, or even running at all, can be as unpredictable as scorching hot days in Britain. The 4.15pm kick-off was also giving me the jitters. If the match went into extra time, followed by a penalty shoot-out, then Wrexham's victory parade, I might not be out of Wembley until very late. Then I would have to navigate the Tube system to get to Euston for my last train back to north Wales.

That's why I ended up watching it at the Wynnstay Arms Hotel in Wrexham. Before booking a table, I'd gone to another large pub in the town and asked the landlord if I could book a table. 'No need,' he blithely replied, 'there'll be no one left in Wrexham on Sunday. They'll all be down at Wembley.' Sadly, I've been born with the kind of mind that, when someone tells me something is categorically so, my brain quickly dredges up the opposite view. The result was I pictured myself in a few days time stuck in a pub filled with large people. I'm pinned against a back wall, catching just the odd glimpse of my heroes on the sacred turf of Wembley. The reason for this partial viewing is that the man in front is about six-foot-four and crashes in at over twenty stone on the scales. OK, I accept I've just been on one of my over-the-top verbal and mental excursions. Now you probably understand why I contacted the Wynnstay and was thrilled that I could easily book a table with an excellent view of the large screen. A table for three in the name of Peter Read. All sorted, no need for any more fears or panics.

When Rona, my brother Jim and I arrived at the hotel in plenty of time for the 4.15pm kick-off, the three of us were chuffed with the positioning of our seats and the fact that we'd have an uninterrupted view of the action from London. Our joy soon came to an abrupt end. A man came to our table. 'You are here to watch the Liverpool/Wolves match, aren't you?'

The staff had decided that because quite a lot of people in Wrexham are Liverpool rather than Wrexham fans, they would give the large area of the bar and the big screen to the Liverpool match. As the man explained, 'After all, it's a vital Premiership match with Liverpool playing Wolves.'

What I wanted to say was, 'Well this is Wrexham after all, not Liverpool. So please put BT Sport on and let us watch our home team.' That's what I wanted to say, but I was too numb with anger to trust what would come out of my mouth once I opened it.

Once I'd composed myself I went to the bar to complain, and explained I'd booked my seats five days before Wrexham's appearance at Wembley. The bar lady used that happy kind of voice most people would reserve for when they are telling someone that he or she has just won millions on the Lottery. 'You can sit down there and watch the Wrexham match. You can choose any seat you want. The screen is set for the match.'

As an act of bravado, or perhaps more accurately a sign of quiet defeat, I went back into the Liverpool wing of the bar and collected the card which had been placed on the table in front of the big screen. I then plonked the card dramatically on the small table where Rona and Jim were sitting: RESERVED FOR PETER READ AND TWO GUESTS.

It would be easy for you to think, 'Good, that's it then. All sorted. They can sit down and enjoy the game.' I suppose that's what I was anticipating, but it was not to be. The area we'd been told to occupy was down some steps from the main area where the Liverpool fans were congregated. Our table was close to the screen, but there was a colossal problem. The commentary was in Welsh, as the TV was on S4C, the Welsh-language channel. It was time for another trip to the bar.

I explained that as I had S4C at home I knew it was possible to press the red button to get English. The young bar staff, who I have to say were extremely helpful and sympathetic to my dilemma, tried several times but were unable to find English commentators. Apparently, S4C were not offering this service for the Buildbase final at Wembley. Not to be undone, I told them that BT Sport was covering the match. It was at that moment I discovered the chilling news that the Wynnstay Arms Hotel did not have BT Sport. By now it was very close to kick-off, far too late to relocate to another bar, which would probably have been packed to the rafters – possibly with everyone watching Wolves and Liverpool rather than Wrexham at Wembley.

There was nothing for it but to sit quietly, admit defeat, keep my mouth shut and watch Wrexham in Welsh. On the scale of Welsh fluency, I suppose I'm between five and six, so I could translate for Jim and Rona, as long as I understood what the commentators were saying. I sipped my beer and decided to behave myself. I'd not utter another word of complaint to the bar staff or anyone within earshot.

The Liverpool match kicked off 15 minutes before Wrexham's final. I slid down into my chair to try and catch what the commentators were saying about Wrexham's chances in the final against Bromley. The loud, raucous racket coming from the other end of the bar from Liverpool fans meant it was impossible to hear a word of the pre-match analysis. It didn't take me too long to break my intended vow of silence. Once again, I was up on my feet at the bar. Obligingly, the young barman turned up the sound. That didn't help much. Although we could now hear our television, coming loud and clear through the loud speaker in our small area of the bar, there was another major problem. The spoken words coming through were nothing to do with the Wrexham match. We were receiving the audio coverage of a completely different programme in English. If I'm not mistaken, it was all about cycling. By now I was too dispirited to climb the steps to what had become the complaints department, also known as the main bar.

My brother Jim, who had come up from Kent to see me for the weekend and was staying at the Wynnstay, suggested we have a look at the TV in his room. There was a bed one of us could sit on, plus two other chairs. He and I went down the corridor into his room. It was hopeless, in a totally different way to the problems we'd encountered at the bar. When the picture decided to grace the screen with its presence, it was excellent. Unfortunately Wembley spent most of its time wobbling.

We trudged back to our seats and watched Wrexham turn in a poor performance and lose 1–0. Despite a world-class save by Bromley's keeper in the dying moments and a goal by Jake Hyde disallowed for a questionable offside decision, plus us hitting the post, we were down and out. Unlike all the fans in the stadium who could live on their memories of the fabulous atmosphere and the great day out they'd enjoyed, we had nothing but tales of television woe to cling on to.

THE PHILOSOPHY OF FOOTBALL FANDOM KICKS IN

Having followed Wrexham for so many years, I have come to the conclusion that after a significant defeat there is a pattern of thought and behaviour that kicks in for the avid fan. First, there is the final whistle syndrome. The ref blows, and after the loss all I can do is sit with my hands covering my mouth. This posture is accompanied by total silence.

This reaction enveloped all three of us. There was no mention of a meal in a restaurant, or a night in and out of various bars supping ale. These had all been mooted before the match. Instead we went our separate ways, and with hugs and few words realised our day of big dreams had just collapsed. But then, even in defeat, there is another syndrome which finds its way into the defeated fan's psyche. This is the 'Find Your Optimism Syndrome'.

It was not long before I was telling myself that I had made the right decision in not going to Wembley. After all, this is a Cup competition, which some would say is not all that important in the wider scale of football triumphs. So it was, in the space of another couple of hours, that I was consoling myself by thinking we would beat Grimsby in the play-off semi-final and then march on West Ham's London Stadium and defeat whoever won the other semi-final. My money was on Solihull Moors.

The final was to be held on 5 June. As luck would have it, I'd be staying in Bedfordshire the week leading up to the final, just an hour's drive from the London Stadium. As you know, as a lifelong fan I've never been too confident about Wrexham in vitally important matches. On this occasion, despite the defeat to Bromley at Wembley, I was supremely confident that whoever we met in the play-off semi-final we would dispatch comfortably. It turned out to be Grimsby Town, who had come from 1–0 down to beat Notts County in extra time.

And so it was that I woke up on 28 May full of optimism, looking forward to the semi-final showdown. We had nothing to fear. Although we'd lost our final league match to Dagenham & Redbridge, I regarded that as a mere blip. Grimsby had had a very mixed season, and after a bright start at the top of the table had slipped quite badly. They had rallied to claim seventh place and earned the right to be in the play-offs. Commentators and the managers of many teams in the Vanarama National League had said that Wrexham and Stockport were the two best teams by a country mile. Besides, Grimsby had only spent one season in the Vanarama National League, whereas we'd been stuck there for 14 years at that point. Surely, they deserved at least five seasons languishing in the depths of football.

About four hours before the 12.30pm kick-off, my calmness was shattered into tiny pieces. The change of mood had nothing to do with football.

When I woke up, my partner was in the bathroom and stayed there for a long time. When she eventually came out she looked ghastly, and her first words were, 'I think I've just had a heart attack.' With pains in her chest and her left arm, she was showing all the signs to suggest her hunch was right. In addition, she was feeling clammy and looked very unwell.

Very quickly a paramedic arrived. By now Rona was feeling a little better and the friendly reassuring paramedic set to work doing loads of tests.

An hour or so into his assessments, he called the

ambulance. While we were waiting he shared some of his lifestory, and it soon became obvious that, like me, he was a follower of Wrexham FC. He was gutted he was working on such an important day in the life of the football club. I asked him what time he was knocking-off, as I now had my ticket and Rona's going spare. Unfortunately for him, he was due to work until 6pm that night. He told me that I might as well go to the match as I would not be able to go into the hospital with Rona. She reiterated the view and said I must go. Much as I wanted to take their advice, I told them I wouldn't feel comfortable doing that.

The ambulance crew arrived and understandably there were more questions to answer, plus more forms to fill in. The paramedic who had been with us all the time was a great character. He winked at the ambulance driver, also a football fan. 'This gentleman,' he said, pointing to me, 'has two tickets for the Wrexham match. If we bump them both up with morphine, we could go to the game, couldn't we?'

Once they had taken Rona to the hospital I had a few things to do to get ready for the match. You guessed right, I eventually took their advice and decided to go to the game. I was delayed by my caring neighbours who wanted to know what had happened. I walked to the ground and have never, in all my days following the team, heard such a cacophony of noise at the Racecourse. Even in the good old days of the great Seventies, in the times of McNeil and Ashcroft and all the others, crowds of 18,000 to 22,000 never matched the glorious racket that was occurring inside the stadium that day. Twelve hundred fans from Grimsby played their part in the sell-out crowd of nearly 10,000.

Sitting in the Wrexham Lager Stand, my whole body tingled from head to toe as I looked around the packed stands and took in the tsunami of audible support. Dafydd Iwan, the Welsh folk singer, was belting out his signature Welsh song, 'Yma o Hyd'. While it's a song about the Welsh nation, it has tremendous significance for the club who nearly went into liquidation, yet were now just two games away from going back into the English Football League. 'Yma o Hyd' means 'Still Here'. Apart from the song's connection to the club and Wales, it also had significance to Rona's situation. She was still here, despite the traumas she'd gone through a few hours before. 'Yma o Hyd.' So poignant and true on so many levels.

While I was pleased to be in my seat, I was naturally concerned about what was going on at the hospital. What I didn't know, until much later, was that Rona was sitting in the ambulance parked in the A&E car park. The football-loving paramedic was still with her. Disappointed she was not getting the benefits from her now redundant ticket, he decided to open the ambulance doors so that they could both soak up the atmosphere, even if it was just through hearing rather than seeing. As the crow flies, it's a very short distance from the hospital to the Racecourse. As well as opening the doors, the paramedic also got the game on his iPad so that they could follow the action.

As far as the game was concerned it was a stunning spectacle if you were a neutral. As you know, I find it difficult to be a neutral in all matters Wrexham. My nerves kicked in when the programme reminded me that the opposition had three ex-Wrexham players in their squad. There is something about footballers who've been rejected by the Reds. When they return to the Racecourse they either have a blinder or score, or both.

In the 13th minute, unlucky for so many, our luck was in when Paul Mullin thrashed the ball from the penalty spot into the net. Our lead lasted just two minutes, when McAtee equalised. At the half-time whistle the score was 1–1. Two minutes into the second half, Grimsby scored. They were now 1–2 up. And their scorer? Well, I did warn you. It was ex-Wrexham player Luke Waterfall. Sixteen minutes later we were level through a Tozer goal, which was only his second of the season. An important goal, which became vital when we edged 3–2 ahead through Paul Mullin's second. Our euphoria lasted just seven minutes, when Taylor scored to make it 3–3. Six minutes later, in the 72nd minute, the earlier euphoria disappeared into despair as Dieseruvwe put Grimsby 3–4 ahead. We needed just two minutes before local hero Jordan Davies from Coedpoeth made it a staggering 4–4 with ten minutes still on the clock. On 90 minutes, the final whistle was blown and we went into extra time. In the 119th minute, with only one minute of extra time remaining, every one in my stand was convinced it would be a penalty shoot-out. Instead, Grimsby snatched the lead to win a pulsating breathless game. And the scorer of the winner? It was that man again, Luke Waterfall, the ex-Wrexham player.

WHAT NOW?

For fans, there is nothing to beat the noise and razzmatazz of people celebrating promotion or a Cup win. The problem was that nearly all the noise was coming from Grimsby fans. Wrexham were making very little noise, just nursing the defeat. There is nothing worse than when your team is relegated, or has missed out on promotion. Fans either sit in total silence staring into space or they wipe away the tears with their Wrexham scarves. When the whistle blew to signal the fact we would be in the Vanarama National League for another season, at least the Grimsby end of our stand erupted into loud shouts and chants of joy.

Needless to say, Wrexham fans sat quietly, privately reliving the nightmare of that final minute of extra time. Then they burst into song to tell the team, 'We love you Wrexham, we do, we love you Wrexham, we do, we love you Wrexham, we do, Oh Wrexham, we love you.' I joined the others, who with blank faces and mouths shut firmly made the long walk into town in near silence. The fans could still be heard affirming their love for the boys in red as the rest of us made our way to pubs, houses, cars, buses or trains.

THE REFEREE

It could be argued that the referee had cost us dearly at Wembley against Bromley. He certainly failed to give us what seemed to be a blatant penalty for a foul on Jordan Davies, and the offside decision for Jake Hyde's goal was also dubious. But that referee's performance faded into insignificance compared to the official handling the game against Grimsby.

The reporter from our local paper is normally very fair and often uses the phrase, 'Referee made a few mistakes but on the whole did well. Six out of Ten', or words to that effect. After the Grimsby match he was not so accommodating, and gave him just two out of ten. Manager Phil Parkinson held nothing back and said:

This division has been great this year. Some good managers, very good players, great attendances. How the League put that referee in charge of this game is absolutely beyond me. I am absolutely seething. Congratulations to Grimsby and good luck in the final. But his performance was so far below the level accepted for a game of this magnitude, it was incredible. If you look at the play-offs in the English Football League, they go for top referees above the standard that they have been refereeing. We had this referee two weeks ago. How he has been put in charge of this game I am absolutely gobsmacked. His performance was beyond belief. We scored a goal which didn't stand, we had a player fouled before their first goal, and we had Bryce Hosannah clattered in the middle of their goal which should have been a penalty. That performance was poor.

Wrexham's *Leader* newspaper, 30 May 2022

I normally give the referee the benefit of the doubt unless he's truly awful, but I have to agree with Phil Parkinson that the ref was worse than awful that day. He was in the realms of disbelief. Of course, it's a thankless task to blow the whistle at any game. I'm reminded of the often-told joke: A referee was getting a torrent of abuse throughout the game. The culprit was standing near the front of the stand. Eventually the man in black had had enough. He went to the fan and said, 'Who's refereeing this game, you or me?' The fan replied, 'Neither of us.'

Fortunately, no player, manager or fan harmed the referee after the Grimsby match. Which is more than can be said about a match in 1912 in the Welsh League between Wattstown and Aberaman Athletic. A player called Hansford, who played for Wattstown, was so angry about the ref's performance that he went into the referee's dressing room to remonstrate with him. It all got out of hand and the player ended up killing him. The footballer was eventually imprisoned for manslaughter. Manslaughter? Was the judge a football fan, I wonder? I guess he must have been, not to find the player guilty of murder and spare him from being hanged.

CHAPTER 8

THOSE INCREDIBLE WREXHAM FANS

NEARLY EVERY FAN of every club in every division is optimistic when the season starts. It's certainly the case with Wrexham fans. If I had a pound for every time a fan has said to me at the beginning of August, 'This is it. It's going to be our season, I'm telling you. This year we're going to get out of this awful league,' I'd be a very rich man.

Then May arrives, carrying with it the end of the season. On the streets of Wrexham you can spot the fans of the home team. They don't need to wear red shirts with Wrexham emblazoned on them. The hangdog look and depressed bearing gives them away. They walk the streets silently, barely speaking to anyone. As they walk they look down at the ground. Are they looking to see if anyone has accidently dropped a season ticket for another club, I wonder?

THE LOYALTY OF FANS

Even before the celebrated Hollywood takeover, the size of crowds watching Wrexham, in what was then a very average league, amazed me. Stuck there for 13 years at that point, they still often pulled in home attendances of 4,000+. Occasionally, the crowd would be around the 6,000 mark, with 8,000 watching a home game against Grimsby and over 9,000 turning up for a first leg play-off match against Kidderminster.

This, in a league where teams such as Boreham Wood, even in seasons where they were doing well, still only had home gates of between 600 and 800.

At a home game I heard one Wrexham fan ask another whether he was going to Dover on Tuesday, and Gateshead on Saturday. The answer was 'yes', so they both looked forward to seeing each other on the bus. Dover is 273 miles away and a four-hour journey, while Gateshead, 193 miles away, is a three-hour trip. That means, by my reckoning, that these two fans, and no doubt many others like them, would in the following week be spending 14 hours on a bus, which is almost the equivalent of two days' work, and would clock up 932 miles in five days to follow their heroes. Of course, they are not alone and it's been my experience following Wrexham that they've always taken a good number of fans to away matches in the Vanarama National League.

The mind starts to boggle when you try and work out how much those Dover and Gateshead trips cost our devoted fans. It also raises another question. Why do so many fans choose to follow Wrexham, when there are at least six Premiership clubs just a 60-minute drive away?

WHY DO WE DO IT?

To answer the question by saying expense is a big factor – given that tickets to watch Premiership matches are extremely expensive, whereas watching non-league football is much kinder on the wallet – doesn't really add up when you start to tot up how much they have to pay to follow the team around Britain.

One answer to the question may be that many feel allegiance to their nearest club. There are, of course, other reasons. Playing in the fifth tier of English football, when Wrexham fans travel away, rather than hatred for the opposition's fans there is a mutual respect. Everyone is in the same fifth-tier boat. It's easy to go into the home team's clubhouse and drink with their fans.

When I was helping Karl Phillips write his book *Bootlegger: The Good, The Bad & The Tasty*, he told me he had videoed Grimsby fans before their FA Trophy final against us and they were incredibly friendly and happy to chat.

He also told me a story that highlights the uncertainty that can sometimes arise with following your team around the country:

> On one occasion, with a couple of mates, we travelled south and booked into a bed and breakfast in Chelmsford so that we'd be nice and fresh for the battle against mighty Braintree the next day. Their ground was just ten minutes away from where we stayed. One hour before kick-off, the match was called off because of the weather. Never mind, just a short, wasted journey of 406 miles there and back.

Colin, of Harlech, drives to every home and away game too. He makes Saturday and midweek matches. When Wrexham are away on Tuesdays he has the little matter of the 70 miles to the Racecourse before starting to try and find Solihull or Maidenhead. As Colin says, 'You shouldn't have to work if you're a Wrexham fan.'

WHERE IS SINCIL BANK?

Bootlegger was fortunate in that he was often given a lift to away games:

> Arriving in Lincoln in August 2013, it didn't take us long to realise we were well and truly lost. The trouble with modern-day cities is that roads through them are generally dual carriageways. It's not like the old days, when you could mount the kerb and nudge the buttocks of a frightened and unsuspecting pedestrian to ask for directions to the football

stadium. It was a good job I wasn't driving, as earlier that season, for a friendly match, I'd jumped into a friend's car expecting a trip to Devon to watch the game. I'd no idea that Tamworth was in the Midlands.

FOREST GREEN, WHO, WHAT, WHERE ARE THEY? (7 SEPTEMBER 2014)

This is still Bootlegger talking, slightly paraphrased and with all the expletives deleted. If I hadn't taken them out I would have gone over the publishers suggested word count massively!

Having struggled to get to Sincil Bank, you'd have thought that to find a team called Forest Green Rovers would have been beyond us. I mean, Lincoln is a well-established city with a cathedral and lots and lots of history. Besides, it's on all the maps in all the atlases. But Forest Green? Where's that? Where do you start to look? Atlases can't help. There's hundreds of forests in England. And, of course, we all know for a fact that nowhere in that country is there a town called Forest Green Rovers. I know where Sherwood Forest is, but after that I'm about as much help as I was in locating Sincil Bank. It's like looking for Albion Rovers, Queen of the South or Hibernian in Scotland. No one knows where they are, except their fans. All I can say is, thank goodness for Georgina and her Sat Nav.

We eventually turned up in a town called Nailsworth in Gloucestershire. I think it's rather cute that Forest Green Rovers play in a stadium called the New Lawn.

I began my vlog with the following greeting to my followers, 'I'm talking to you through the eye of a net at the New Lawn. It's the best bit of grass I've seen since I was in my mate's attic last week.'

The influence of owner Dale Vince's beliefs can be seen in

the fact that one of the stands has 180 solar panels on the roof. This helps to generate ten per cent of the electricity needed to run the stadium. In 2012, a year after Vince took over the club, Forest Green Rovers became the first British football club to use a robot lawn mower on its pitch. The Etesia robot ETMower, known as Mow Bot, uses GPS technology to guide it around without the need for human intervention and gathers power from the stadium's solar panels.

Think about it. Instead of investing in lawn mowers, what would happen if Wrexham bought into this robot idea and managed to sneak in a few robot players. Strikers, of course. Goal Bots instead of Mow Bots. Never again would a glorious ball split the opposition's defence, 'with no Wrexham player within a million miles of the ball'. GPS would make sure that our leading Bot was in the right place at the right time to boot the ball into the top corner of the net, or wherever inside the net the technology wanted it to be.

Dream on, Wrexham. I think that's definitely one for the future!

A FEW FANS TELL IT AS IT IS

Addicted

An illness refusing to go away.
Of all the strains I could have caught,
Man Utd, Man City, Liverpool or Everton,
I go down with Long Wrexhamitis.

The first match, like the first kiss,
never ever to be forgotten.

The pitch flat as a grass billiard table,
its brilliant green illuminating
the drab grey of this northern town.

Looking down from steep terraces,
the match is human chess.
Defenders are pawns, wingers rooks,
the keepers protected kings. The team
pushing up, pulling back, stretching
the board as far as it will go.

Then checkmate. Goal.
Magic. Call it what you will.

The walk to bus, car, train, pub, or home.
'Experts' dissect the story, arthritic limbs
mimic remembered moves. Smiling faces
dream of their next Wrexham football fix.

That's something I prepared a little earlier. In fact, I wrote it a long time before Rob and Ryan took over the club. It was originally commissioned, with other footy poems from other writers, for an evening of sporting poems at the Carnival of Words, an annual literature festival in Wrexham. The event was staged at Saith Seren, the Welsh translation of its previous name, the Seven Stars.

Although it's my own personal view of being severely addicted to the weekly bag of wind being passed and kicked around, it can apply to so many of the fans who have followed the Reds. It would be impossible to feature every one of the 9,000 or so faithful who turn out in all types of weather to all kinds of places to chant for the club.

In this next section I have restricted myself to people I know. If I tried to cover every sector of fan I fear we would need a set of at least ten books. That's my defence for the fact that while I mention and applaud the thousands of fans who form a regular and dependable group of supporters every week, the following people are inevitably male and also roughly my age.

COLIN BOOTE

On a Saturday in April 2022, I was in Tŷ Pawb, the Wrexham arts hub, as part of the literature festival there. Colin was walking through on his way to Wrexham's penultimate home match of a season. To watch Wrexham play most of their home games, I'd personally travel on foot no more than a season's total of 46 miles – one mile there, one mile back. By contrast, Colin travelled thousands of miles in the 2021–22 season.

Although originally from the Wrexham area, for many years he has lived in Epsom in Surrey. With 15 of the 23 teams in the 2021–22 Vanarama National League based in the south, Wrexham's fixture list posed interesting challenges for Colin. So-called home matches were a mammoth journey from Surrey to north Wales, while some of the grounds which were horrendous journeys for Wrexham fans were closer to being home matches for him. Even with the bonus of living in the south, he still managed to clock-up 16,000 miles in the season watching the boys in red.

When I initially told him I figured his 16,000-mile pilgrimages to watch Wrexham meant that he must have spent two weeks and one hour just travelling to the matches, he was amazed. So dumbfounded was he that he decided to do his own calculations. Surely he hadn't spent 337 hours in the car? He was right to check as my figures were wrong. He'd actually been car-bound for 390 hours. And that's without adding the hours spent listening to Wrexham podcasts and watching TV highlights.

Home games are really like away trips for him. As he says, it's just as well that he is self-employed. It's also just as well that his wife Alison accompanies him to many of the games. Even Bob, their Welsh Border Collie, came with them to watch Wrexham away on one occasion in 2018. Colin and Alison heard that Guiseley FC welcomed dogs to matches, as the club's mascot is an English Mastiff.

Before I take my statistical hat off, you might like to

know how 16,000 miles translates into other journeys. When making crossings across the Pond to watch some of the matches at the Racecourse, Rob and Ryan have a 5,276-mile flight from Los Angeles. As Wrexham is 2,553 miles from the North Pole, you could say that Colin's support has been the rough equivalent of six to seven trips to the North Pole or three flights to Los Angeles. And there's me boasting when I've made away trips to distant places such as Chester, Bolton and Cardiff! There have been many others over the years, although I guess if they were all added up together they wouldn't get within a sniff of 16,000 miles.

The love affair with all things Wrexham FC started for Colin in September 1967 at the age of eight. Taken by his father and uncle, the match was memorable for at least three reasons. There was such a large crowd for the game against Hartlepool that there were massive queues outside to get into the ground. While the three were waiting to be allowed in, they heard two huge roars. Wrexham's two opening goals had been scored while Colin and many other fans were still outside. Secondly, it was the first time Colin caught sight of the talents which were Ray Smith, Arfon Griffiths and Albert Kinsey. Despite getting in late, he saw enough of the game to be hooked for life. And thirdly, Wrexham thrashed the north-east team, 6–0.

Strangely, I also remember that game very well, although I never saw it. The late Sixties and early Seventies marked the ultra religious stage of my life. I must confess that I was gutted not to be there. The other difficulty about that afternoon was that the Christian conference I attended was within earshot of the ground, and every now and again I could hear raucous football roars from the Racecourse. Were they goals or just near misses? I had no idea. I slipped out of the church on the pretence that I needed the loo. My watch told me that the ref should have blown full-time, and that by now fans should be filing past the building. I and the watch were right. I asked someone the score and was thrilled that we had found the back of the net six times without reply.

Colin was too young to be able to afford to travel to places such as Zürich, Djurgårdens or Hajduk Split, but saw many of the great European tussles at home. Despite watching some crack European sides at the Racecourse, his most memorable match was at White Hart Lane against Tottenham Hotspur in the League Cup. Bizarrely, like the Hartlepool match just mentioned, I also remember that Spurs game very well.

I was still in the sixth form and it was half-term. In those days many grocers and butchers used to sell their groceries or meat by driving around council estates blasting their horns. Housewives would come out and buy what they wanted. It was often cheaper than buying from the shops. On the afternoon of the Spurs match, 'Roger' was making his way around the estate where I lived. Roger was not his proper name. That name has been given to him in the interests of protecting the guilty rather than the innocent. When he saw me he slowed down and asked if I wanted to go with him to the away match at White Hart Lane.

Roger drove around in a very dodgy and dangerous-looking van. It was too old to be offered to a museum! In addition, to open the passenger's door and get inside you needed to be a contortionist. As I considered what to do, there were two factors that encouraged me to stay in Wrexham. As I've already said, I was 18 and more than likely still had a future ahead of me. It might not be glittering, but it could still be some kind of future. The other fact that screamed stay put was that the vehicle that was going to take me to England's capital city would probably have lost its door by the time we got to Telford.

The next morning I heard the exciting, yet slightly disappointing result. Disappointing, because I could have been present to witness one of Wrexham's great victories against opposition from the then First Division, now the

103

Premiership. Colin Boote had been excited watching the match, and it's little wonder that he rates it as one of the most memorable games in all his years watching the team. It wasn't just the fact that Wrexham won 2–3 against all the odds that has stayed embedded in his memory. It was also a never-to-be-forgotten journey home for all the wrong reasons.

Spurs fans attacked their bus as it tried to get out of London. Many of the windows were smashed, so the jubilant fans headed back up to Wrexham without all the windows. Imagine what it must have been like for Colin and the other passengers driving up the M1 that September 1976 evening. No doubt the chanting and the singing kept them warm.

As Colin looked back at the first full season of Hollywood stars in charge, he was aware that the football he'd watched was so different to what he'd witnessed during the previous seasons in the fifth tier:

> When I first heard that they were taking over I was overcome with sheer disbelief. I've not met them, but the way they've integrated into the town and the club is sheer class.
>
> I can't imagine any other new owners could have made themselves so popular so quickly. They've given us hope and belief again. Their commitment is infectious. The biggest positive of their takeover will be the way they energise the young supporters who'll see them as role models. Their worldwide reach is going to be massive for the club and we'll have to deal with being in the spotlight a whole lot more.
>
> It's so different watching them now compared to seasons ago. There's now an expectation that we'll get ahead, even if we fall behind. The best example of that was against Dover in the 2021–22 season, when we were losing 2–5 with about 20 minutes to go and we won 6–5.

STEVE AND NIGE

Steve Duckett and Nigel Rowland were in the same year as me at Ysgol Rhiwabon. After losing touch for many years, we renewed contact when I returned to live in Wrexham in 2010. Before the Dagenham home match in the 2020–21 season, they came round to my house for a few nibbles and goodly quantities of the red stuff. Between munching and slurping, I was keen to know what they made of the new owners and the progress so far. For Steve, home matches could be a marathon journey as he lives near Wakefield. Not as challenging as Colin Boote's journeys, but still a long trek. I was keen to chat with them, as they've clocked up far more games than me at the Racecourse and from watching Wrexham away from home. Despite living in West Yorkshire, Steve has had a season ticket for several seasons.

STEVE: At the moment I'm riding the wave. Just hoping it carries us to the right place.

NIGE: When you think that just before the Covid lockdown we were in real danger of being relegated to the league below us. Whatever happens in the next few years, it has to better than that prospect.

STEVE: Before Rob and Ryan took over I seriously considered throwing in the towel. I was ready to stop my long association with the club. The fan base seemed more concerned with eating each other alive than getting behind the team.

NIGE: People in the stands and all around the ground seemed to be resigned to the fact that we were going down. The quietness at matches was overwhelming. It was difficult to believe that 3,000 to 4,000 fans could make so little noise.

STEVE: All I can say to Rob and Ryan is, 'Thanks for giving us so much hope.'

NIGE: So far the two stars have started delivering on everything they promised in their mission statement.

STEVE: It's so great that, at the moment, the chat among

fans is about the elements of the football being served up, rather than everyone attacking those trying to run the club.

NIGE: You can tell that the vast majority of fans are happy. We're happy now, but I'm sure we'll all be liable to massive mood swings after some results.

STEVE: This takeover is not only important for the die-hard fans, it's also going to be vital for the town. I'm sure these A-Listers will unlock potential all around this area.

NIGE: It's not just that the feel-good factor is back for everyone. The names of Ryan and Rob are plastered everywhere, but then so is the name of our town, Wrexham.

STEVE: Is there a slag heap safe from publicity I wonder, as everyone jumps on the bandwagon?

While my two friends were positive about what had happened and hopeful about the future, they were concerned about the midfield. The two main strikers at that time, Jake Hyde and Paul Mullin, had to work too hard to get the ball. Their feeling was that since Lee Fowler had left the club, successive managers had failed to address this problem. When John Rooney was forced to play in a traditional midfield line-up, his undoubted talents were being wasted. This resulted in far too many players hoofing the ball in the general direction of the strikers, probably with the accompaniment of a muffled prayer as they hoped to God that the 'wellied' pass would find one of the two strikers. Needless to say, this act of intercession was rarely rewarded, as those of us who watched them for years can testify. It was crying out for someone to play just behind the front two. It could be claimed that this wasn't fully solved until the arrival of Elliot Lee in the 2022–23 season.

In the 2021–22 season Steve had suggested to his wife Ros that she might like to accompany him to watch Wrexham's away game against Grimsby Town (who play at Cleethorpes). At first his wife was not enthusiastic. In fact she was positively against the idea. She reminded Steve that the only time she'd accompanied him to watch Wrexham away they had ended up sitting next to two foul-mouthed women who swore profusely for most of the 90 minutes. And they weren't just small swear words, either. Those two had gone in for expletives from the top division of obscenities. After Steve's gentle persuasion and his statement that it was highly unlikely they would ever see those two fans again, Ros gave in and agreed to go with him to the match. In their seats before the game, waiting for the teams to take to the pitch, Steve was slightly amazed. Was it? Surely it couldn't be. Sadly it was. The two who'd made their lives so miserable during Ros' one and only away game at Lincoln City were in the same stand clutching tickets looking for their seats. Steve consoled himself that the chances of them having tickets in the seats next to him and his wife were slim. In fact they were sadly very high, and eventually the two women plonked themselves next to them. One of the women told Steve that Cleethorpes was near Blackpool and the next time the Reds played Grimsby she and her friend would stay in the area for some extra days at Blackpool. Steve pointed out the Cleethorpes was near Lincoln and was on the east coast, whereas Blackpool was in the north-west. Steve worked hard at pointing out the errors of her geography, but she was having none of it. As far as she was concerned, she was right and he was wrong. As well as her getting that wrong, the evening delivered the wrong result, as Wrexham lost 3–1.

Having watched Wrexham avidly for many years at home and at many away matches, of all the memories Nige stored away there were two that surfaced to the top. He and two friends drove down to Bournemouth to watch Wrexham.

It was a New Year's Day match with an afternoon kick-off. They decided to drive down the day before and spent the night in a Shaftesbury car park. When they woke up in the morning they tried to work out what had happened in the dead of night. How had they been transported from a car into an ice box? They feared that the ice had stuck their bodies to the car seats. The temperature that night had sunk to –10°c and Nige and his friends spent the day thawing out, ready for kick-off. Before the match they were outside Dean Court, as the Bournemouth ground was then called, in time to see the Wrexham team arrive in their warm coach. Armed with the confidence that came from their night-long ordeal, Nige decided to approach the bus. Having asked Albert Kinsey whether he had any free tickets to spare, he went on to explain that they had driven down the day before and slept in the car, in which they nearly froze to death. Albert's response was to say, 'You must all be fucking mad.'

Those were the days, of course, when Wrexham were in the Football League. Nige plucks his other memory from non-league days. With his son Mike, he went to see Wrexham play Guiseley. They arrived nice and early, and as they were walking around the ground he froze and grabbed his son's arm. Alluding to the area of the ground in which they were heading, he pointed to a huge creature that had its paws over the wall.

'It's a lion,' said Nige.

'Have you been taking drugs?'

Eventually Nige, with the help of his son, plucked up the courage to move towards the 'Beast of Guiseley'. We have already mentioned that Guiseley FC were animal friendly, but allowing lions to sit in the front row of their stadium seems to be stretching the policy a little too far. Once they got within shooing distance of the creature, they both agreed it was the largest dog either of them had ever seen. In addition, its 'mane' had for some reason been dyed purple.

Just as there were problems at the Guiseley match, watching the team in the Wrexham Lager Stand didn't get off to the best of starts, either. With his season ticket he took his usual seat for the match against Notts County. That night the stand was jam-packed due to the fact that the WREXRENT

Stand was not ready and the attendance had been reduced to around 5,000. Behind Nige, two older fans saw the match as an opportunity to outdo each other on facts about football in general, and Wrexham Football Club in particular. Unfortunately, the man directly behind Nige had no teeth. This meant that he spat his answers to his friend's questions on to the back of Nige's neck. As the game wore on, the other said to him, 'I'll be glad when we get our seats back in the WREXRENT Stand.' Nige resisted the temptation to stand up, turn around and say, 'So will I.'

DAVE SUBACCHI

Dave Subacchi worked for many years as a civil servant with Wrexham County Borough Council. I often bump into him in the upper Wrexham Lager Stand. Interestingly, the first time he saw Wrexham play he was shouting for the wrong team. I will let him tell his story in his own words:

We got the train to Wrexham from Aberystwyth, via Shrewsbury, for the evening kick-off. It was 7 February 1972. Half the town came with us to see the Seasiders play the Robins in the Welsh Cup sixth round. It was a long journey there and even longer coming back as Wrexham beat us, 6–2.

Before the match we spilled into a little pub with a thatched roof, but we didn't like the lager and a sign below the low ceiling which read, 'No foreign cigarettes, please.' We were to taste disappointment, too.

At the Racecourse we marvelled at the size of the place and the crowd lit-up by the great floodlights. I had never seen such a sight or heard so great a roar. We did all that we could do. Wrexham gave us a hiding, though we were not disgraced. We left with our heads held high, and as our train pulled out I recall something struck the carriage window. It was a red Ruabon brick.

You might be asking yourself, 'What on earth is an Aberystwyth fan doing on the pages of a book dedicated to the wonders of following Wrexham?' In case you are contemplating putting the book down, let me leap to Dave's defence. In 1989, when Brian Flynn became manager, Dave moved to Wrexham and has followed them ever since.

As we talk, it becomes clear that Dave is not an aficionado when it comes to recalling matches he's seen. For him, the spectacle of a football game is everything that goes with a day-out at the Racecourse. He can often recall the excellent bowl of chips he consumed before kick-off, or the pint or two he quaffed after the final whistle. Then he tells me about a game he saw. He remembers it ended 2–1 but he can't remember who won or who lost because he has forgotten who was playing. One thing he does recall is that a streaker ran on to the pitch. I should point out that Dave is a first-class poet, with books of poems to his name, so no doubt his mind is on higher things.

In fairness to Dave he does not forget details of all the games he has watched. When asked which was the best game he had ever seen, there is no hesitation as he tells me it had to be Wrexham playing Arsenal in the third round of the FA Cup. He can even remember the date, 4 January 1992, and has written a poem about the day which he read out at a football poetry evening at Saith Seren.

While that was a golden moment for Dave, there are games that stick in his memory for different reasons. The first was a derby match at the Racecourse between Wrexham and Chester:

I didn't intend going, but the smell of chips drove me there.
It's hard to explain, but a Wrexham v Chester game is
something special. I bought a pound cone of chips with lots
of vinegar, and walked past police from both sides of the
border hiding in corners. For some reason, the derby game
kicked-off at 2pm. I was too late for a ticket. Guard dogs

growled, a steward sighed. Wind blew through the old Kop now long closed, but still full of ghosts, waiting patiently for better times. Back in the centre of the grey half-empty town, I bought more chips, with a pie, too, and a pint of the local stuff.

JOHN THE BELL
At Gresford church they put the bell on his coffin
and rang it at the end of the service.
You must remember John the Bell,
at home and away games he would ring out
during moments of tension or when spirits
needed to be lifted, ding-dong. 'It's John the Bell.'
'Why is he ringing?' 'What does he mean by it?'
'Why doesn't he shut up?' 'No, I like it.'
'C'mon Wrexham.' 'That's John the Bell.'
'Good old John – ring that bloody bell.'
'C'mon Wrexhaaaaaaaaaaaaaaaaaaam!'
At a Cup tie against Newcastle
the Geordies stole the bell.
But the black-and-white seas parted
as John entered the pub
to recover his prized possession.
The Toon Army surrendered,
offering little opposition.
Even in Europe the Bell was heard.
We would catch it on radio and TV.
Wherever Wrexham played
John the Bell was there.
To many he was 'John the Butcher' too,
in the market and then in Henblas Street.
The meat sales continue
but the bell-ringing has ended,
and the closed-down Kop where he stood
awaits future redevelopment.
Some like to think that's where
all the Wrexham fans stand

that have all passed on, and if that's true
John the Bell is with them,
ringing as they cheer us on.

David Subacchi
(17 December 2014)

MARK NICHOLLS

These are Mark Nicholls' recollections:

I began watching Wrexham at the age of seven. My father
used to take me to the home games. He'd drive from
Queens Park and leave the car in East Avenue, Rhosddu. In
the winter and at evening matches, you'd see the massive
floodlights from a long way away, towering over the town.
We'd stand behind the Kop goal, where we'd often meet
up with my teenage cousin Terry, who now lives in Perth,
Australia, and still follows Wrexham from there.

My idol was the great Eddie May. What a leader! A
majestic centre-half with shoulders the size of a brick
outhouse. Another favourite was Billy Ashcroft, a burly
ginger-haired Liverpudlian. The special time for me was a
home 7–1 win against Rotherham Utd in 1978 which helped
seal promotion from the old Third Division to the Second
Division, what is now called the Championship. But then
there were the nights at the European Cup Winners' Cup
on four separate occasions. It saw tales of famous victories,
dodgy refereeing, trips across the Iron Curtain, and most
memorably a run to the quarter-finals in 1976, when only
Anderlecht, a team packed full of world-class stars, prevented
further glory for us.

Our first venture to foreign fields was in 1972. A Welsh
Cup win over Cardiff saw us qualify, and we made our
European debut against FC Zürich. Albert Kinsey scored
Wrexham's first European goal in a 1–1 draw in Switzerland,
before the tie was then won on an emotional night in front

of 18,000 fans at the Racecourse. Reds legends Billy Ashcroft and Mel Sutton got the goals to clinch a 2–1 victory for John Neal's men. Our European adventures were up and running. The next round saw us paired up with the Yugoslavian outfit Hajduk Split – with our home leg first. Eventually, we lost to an away goal. I distinctly remember the radio commentary saying there were some terrible refereeing decisions from the Polish referee.

Maybe the greatest memory of mine was the game against Anderlecht. In my opinion they were the best opposition to grace the hallowed turf of the Racecourse. Rob Rensenbrink was a player who'd just glide past players when in full flow, but Mickey Evans and Alan Hill (whom I played with during our amateur days) would work tirelessly to keep him quiet, but all he needed was the one chance, then the inevitable happened. These nights were special times in which my dad and I formed a great bond. Those experiences made me the person I am today.

The memorable FA Cup runs were family affairs to watch, when brothers, cousins and uncles would take in the smoke-filled air around the Kop. Arfon Griffiths, the midfield general, would often be the star, with the likes of Mel Sutton and Les Cartwright running the channels. In the 2000s, my nieces Charlotte and Courtney used to go with their dad Brian. They idolised Lee Trundle, and what a player he was. Neil Roberts graced that team and he went on to play for Wigan Athletic. The day Mickey Thomas scored the goal against Arsenal in the FA Cup, I was in transit to Australia with work, and caught the highlights in Singapore. What a time!

Nowadays I spend match days with my brothers Lawrence and Lance, stepson Jamie, and my nephews Harri, James, Dylan, Rhaeadr, and now the youngest, Carter, is getting involved, This current team is building another proud legacy spurred on by this great club. This present season has brought me closer to old friends and family as I travel across the UK to watch Wrexham AFC.

We have been Wrexham AFC supporters since 1921. Sadly, in 1934, the bodies of three family members were eternally incarcerated in the Gresford mine disaster. They had swapped shifts that day so that they could take in the fixture at home against Tranmere Rovers. They were Harry, John, and William H Nicholls.

Mark's poignant telling of his story is very moving and a great example of a family who continued watching and supporting Wrexham through different generations.

***

ALL SHAPES, SIZES AND AGES OF FANS

I've already explained why, at half-time, I rarely venture down to the food places or toilets. It's too much of a physical battle. Instead, when the half-time whistle blows I indulge in people watching. Having thought of individual fans and their tales of following the team, I realise that at every game for a couple of hours I look out on a sea of faces and shapes. Every particle of that ocean has its own story to tell, its reason for being there.

There are people who caught the bug from their now deceased father. Or people who were given the baton of adulation for the team and now pass it on to their own children. There are the slightly bemused, who having read the papers have come to see what all the fuss is about. Then there are those who played the game professionally or at amateur level. These can be separated from those who've hardly ever kicked a ball, except in their back yard when they were growing up. The latter tend to shout at the players during the match, swear profusely when someone in the team makes a mistake, never chant or applaud, just tut-tut their frustration and try to enlist the support of those sitting around them. On the whole, those who have played and know the game tend to watch in silence. Aware that there are times when players just can't get into a game and the ball passes them by, they conceal their frustration created by the 'know it all, know nothing really fans'.

Of course, professors and academics have written learned tomes about the sociology and psychology of the average football fan. As I say, I'm just an observer indulging my passion for people watching. It only takes a few minutes after kick-off for the referee haters to emerge in the crowd. They delight in telling the man in green, or whatever colour he wears these days, through enough loud shouts to encourage others with a similar view, 'You don't know what you're doing!'

I often wonder what's going on in such a fan's mind. Has the man in black – sorry habits die hard and I still think of the referee in that way – morphed into the man's boss? Is it that the venom hissing its way to the official is something the fan would love to dump on his manager first thing on Monday morning? Or has the referee suddenly changed, and is he now receiving all the hidden angst the man wishes he could send to his wife or partner?

Inevitably, in crowds of 9,000 or more, there will be plenty of conspiracy theorists. If Wrexham are struggling out there on the pitch, these fans will tell anyone who will listen – or more accurately has to listen because they're sitting next to them – a version of the following: 'I've had it on good authority from people in high places at the club, that they don't want to go up. If they get back into the English Football League Division Two they'll go straight down. The crowds will disappear and they won't have money to buy decent players. Then the slide will continue and they'll eventually end up playing at a small ground in the Welsh League with crowds of 1,000 or less.' This conspiracy is always wheeled out when Wrexham lose in a play-off match and are banished to yet another season in the Vanarama National League.

Over the years I have sat in different parts of the ground

for different matches. Some people attend matches who, while they are ardently shouting for Wrexham, know very little about the history of the team or even the names of the current squad. They are likely to ask someone sitting near them for a loan of their match-day programme so they can work out who just missed a sitter or who's been sent off. I have no problem with such people. Their lack of knowledge about the intricacies of the team or the club's history probably means that, unlike me, they live balanced lives.

THE FAIR-WEATHER BRIGADE

Of course, when the team is doing well the attendances suddenly shoot up. This is certainly true since the Hollywood stars took over. The rise in attendances from between 3,000 and 4,000 pre-2020 Covid to crowds in excess of 8,000, sometimes topping 9,000 or 10,000, has been astronomical. This transformation is welcomed by the backroom staff who run the club and see the money rolling in through the turnstiles, but it's not a view shared by some sections of the crowd. These are the die-hard fans, the fans who remember the bad old days when, after a crowd of over 12,000 watched Wrexham gain an honourable draw against Real Zaragoza in the European Cup Winners' Cup, they were there the next Saturday to watch Wrexham take on Aldershot in the fourth tier. The gate for that match numbered just over 1,000 people, a meagre attendance to say the least. These people stand with disbelief and derision etched on their faces. 'Where were they in the bad old days when we needed them most?' they ask their equally disgruntled friend, who nods his head in agreement. In the early days of the Gary Mills era, when Wrexham were playing well and with high hopes of being promoted that season, the woman selling the 50/50 tickets outside the ground berated me for being a fair-weather fan. Of course I wasn't. I got to most of the home games. It was just she hadn't seen me before.

STATISTICS BUFFS

Within every crowd there are plenty of statistic buffs. They are ready to pounce with a correction if you are wrong about any detail of the current game. They are also quite happy to give you the right details if you venture into results and names of players from previous seasons. I am in awe of such people. In fact I have to admit there is something of the 'correct statistics please syndrome' in my make up. Admittedly, my strength in that department is grounded in the years before Wrexham slipped into non-league. I'm pretty strong on the facts from 1962 right up to 2008 when we ended up in non-league. Sadly, for the 15 seasons in the Vanarama National League (or its previous names), I'm poor. It's as if when people take me into that territory I suffer from post-traumatic shock disorder. I try hard to forget everything from that period of football history.

During the 2021–22 season in the Wrexham Lager Stand, behind where I sat were two young boys, Stefan and Aled, and their father Gavin. Aled was eight and Stefan was 12. I used to listen to them with amazement. In terms of football, nothing seemed to be out of their grasp. I ended up asking their father if it would be alright if ever I ended up on the TV programme *Who Wants to Be a Millionaire?* that I gave their names to the producers of the show, just in case I needed to phone a friend about football.

CHAPTER 9

THE CROWDS, THE CROWDS, WHEREVER YOU LOOK, CROWDS!

FOR RYAN AND Rob's first full season in charge of the club, Wrexham finished top of the Vanarama National League table in terms of home attendances.

HOME CROWDS, VANARAMA NATIONAL LEAGUE, 2021-22 SEASON

	CAPACITY	SPECTATORS	AVERAGE	PERCENTAGE
WREXHAM	15,500	190,232	8, 647	55.8%
STOCKPORT	10,832	156,761	7,126	65.8%
NOTTS CO	21,388	149,592	6,800	31.8%
CHESTERFIELD	10,504	140,859	6,403	61.0%
SOUTHEND	12,392	127,013	5,773	46.4%
GRIMSBY	9,546	125,683	5,713	59.9%
WOKING	6,064	58,597	2,664	43.9%
EASTLEIGH	3,000	56,462	2,556	85.6%
TORQUAY	6,104	55,400	2,518	41.3%
YEOVIL	9,527	52,378	2,378	25.0%

HALIFAX	14,061	48,870	2,130	15.2%
ALTRINCHAM	6,085	46,612	2,119	34.8%
BROMLEY	5,000	43,172	1,962	39.3%
ALDERSHOT	7,100	40,123	1,824	25.7%
SOLIHULL	5,500	39,130	1,779	32.3%
DAGENHAM	6,000	39,036	1,774	30.3%
MAIDENHEAD	4,000	31,004	1,409	35.2%
WEALDSTONE	4,085	29,539	1,407	34.4%
WEYMOUTH	6,600	25,870	1,176	17.8%
KINGS LYNN	8,200	25,477	1,158	14.1%
BOREHAM WOOD	4,502	23,275	1,058	23.5%
DOVER	6,500	16,600	830	12.8%

It's amazing to see that ten of the 22 teams in the Vanarama National League attracted average crowds of under 2,000 throughout the season. When you take into account the six big guns, Wrexham, Stockport County, Notts County, Chesterfield, Southend and Grimsby, who would have taken a large contingent of their own fans to these grounds – probably giving the home club their highest home attendances – it makes you realise how huge the gulf is.

In addition, whoever compiled this list took Wrexham's ground capacity as 15,500, which is the projected figure for when the new stand is finally erected on the site of the old Kop. If Wrexham's current capacity of 10,000 had been used, the percentage attendance would have been much higher than the stated 55.8 per cent.

For all the years that I've followed Wrexham in the National League, it's always been the case that only one club gets automatic promotion, while the second-placed team has to slog it out in the lottery known as the play-offs. We Wrexham fans, and I'm sure many fans of other National League clubs, have wondered why this is the situation. Is it that the powers-that-be are convinced that there are not enough good teams in the lower league to hold their own in League Two of the English Football League? Teams such as Burton Albion, Salford, Fleetwood, Crawley and many more have already disproved that particular view.

Or perhaps the idea from years ago prevails, that the National League teams are poorly supported, and if two made their way automatically to League Two each season their poor attendances would reflect badly on the English Football League. The figures in the table disprove that view. It's also worth noting that in the 2021–22 season, the top seven teams in the National League had higher average home attendances than all those who finished between fifth and 24th in League Two. Nine teams in the bottom half of that league attracted crowds ranging from 2,781 down to 2,126. Of all the teams in that division it could be argued that only Bradford City stood out, with crowds averaging 15,000. The four other teams in the top five were Swindon (average crowd 9,449), Bristol Rovers (7,500), Port Vale (6,189) and Northampton Town (5,366). All these statistics suggest that many Vanarama National League teams could hold their own in the English Football League. Interestingly, the figures for the bottom nine clubs in League One for season 2021–22 had average gates which were all less than the top six in the National League.

At the time of writing in 2023, the debate is still raging regarding the possibility of two National League clubs being automatically promoted to League Two. It's good to see that Rob and Ryan have added their weight to the demand for change, as has the *Non-League Football Paper*. We can but wait, dream and hope.

CHAPTER 10

WHAT ROB AND RYAN HAVE DONE FOR THE CLUB AND TOWN

OFTEN, WHEN MEGA-RICH people take over the ownership of a football club, they turn up for the first game and are then rarely seen for the rest of the season. Ryan and Rob certainly do not match that caricature. From their first visit to Wrexham in October 2021 for the Torquay home match, it was clear they had every intention of relating with the fans and inhabitants of Wrexham. Drinks at the Turf, walks along the streets to greet locals, plus many free bottles of Aviation American Gin assured fans that these were no distant owners barely interested in those who pay money to watch the team. They kept saying they were here for the duration, in the hope of turning this National League side into a global presence. In the early days of their takeover, Ryan joked that the two owners would be so involved in the life of the town that we would get sick and tired of them. Two years on, I would say there is little likelihood of that happening.

After two years at the helm, Ryan was able to share his great love for the team and city of Wrexham with a reporter from the *Metro* newspaper:

This isn't hyperbole when I say it's been the great privilege of my life to be part of this project, and something I'm quite sure I'll be a part of until the day I close my eyes on this weird, dumb show. I've enjoyed every second of it. Not just the football club, but the community of Wrexham, the way they've embraced Rob and me.

It certainly was an unorthodox kind of proposition when we came in but, putting community first, we didn't really necessarily come in with that ethos.

They taught us that – when we looked at the community. So it has been a really beautiful experience, top to bottom. Win or lose. We just love every aspect of this community and this club.

SUPPORTING INDIVIDUALS

Both owners have shown real concern and have linked up with local individuals. This is evident not only from helping those who are in need of financial help, but also from supporting those who aim to raise money for worthy causes. Paul Edwards, from Penycae near Wrexham, is a well-known character and a superlative fundraiser. In early 2023 he set off on a mammoth walking trip to raise money for the Wrexham hospice, Hope House / Tŷ Gobaith. His 3,000-mile walk took in California and treks through New Mexico, Texas, Oklahoma, Arkansas, Tennessee, Mississippi, Alabama and Georgia. The aim of this epic walk was to raise a total of £20,000 for the charity. One day, sitting outside a café, the GPS linked to his phone buzzed with a message. He began to think that the message was a wind-up – maybe one of his friends back in Wrexham pretending to be Ryan Reynolds. But no, this really was Ryan Reynolds. As well as messaging Paul to wish him every success with his walk, Ryan also promised him a new phone so that he could keep in touch with his Wrexham friends, especially those at the Turf pub.

It's not just members of the community for whom the two co-owners show concern and support. In the 2021–22 season, Tyler French was a very polished and effective player who often took over at the back when Aaron Hayden was injured. He made a total of 38 appearances for the north Wales club.

Released by Wrexham, he eventually signed for Dundee in the second tier of the Scottish League. Playing against St Mirren on 21 January 2023, he sustained a horrific injury and was carried off. Later that evening, Tyler tweeted, 'Thank you for all the messages. Unfortunately, not great news but I'll be back better and stronger as soon as possible.' Rob McElhenney replied, 'Tyler, I am so sorry. Get well soon. Pulling for you always.'

In February 2023 cyclists prepared for a race which involved cycling 555 miles from Cardiff to Edinburgh in 48 hours. The race was in memory of the famous Scottish rugby player Doddie Weir, and the prize was the Doddie Weir Cup. There were 200 cycle teams involved and 38,000 fundraisers. Ryan Reynolds cheered on and sponsored the Glenkinchie team of riders. The ride raised money for the Motor Neurone Disease Society, which supports those with the crippling disease that Doddie suffered and ultimately died from. Ryan wrote: 'This is a message for the entire team in this incredible MND ride. I just wanna wish you guys all the best – go get 'em! What an incredible cause. It's a great thing you're all doing. I hear you may stop off at the Racecourse Ground, so enjoy it. It's a pretty magical place and best of luck to each and every one of you.'

As we have seen in a previous chapter, there are quite a few people in the Wrexham area who have been helped by the kindness and financial help of Rob and Ryan.

WREXHAM, FROM A PLACE TO AVOID TO A PLACE TO VISIT

I was born in Rhosllanerchrugog, and while this section is on the subject of Wrexham's identity, perhaps it's important to linger for a moment on the fact that, just as in the past, Wrexham has had problems in defining itself – my birthplace certainly suffered similar difficulties. The powers-that-be and the sign writers who create the big signs saying 'Welcome to Wherever' were not sure whether my home village had one 'n' or two. The makers of signs on the A483 road approaching Wrexham from the Shrewsbury or Oswestry direction found that their sign was not big enough to accommodate every letter for the turn off to Rhosllanerchrugog. At one stage in the dual carriageway's history, they split the village's name into three. A friend of mine once texted me to get directions, as he wanted to know whether I lived in Rhos, Llanerch or Rugog.

On my visits to Wrexham when I was a boy I was conscious of the fumes from cars in the crowded roads, as in those days there were few pedestrian walkways. The only places you could feel safe were on cramped pavements, and if someone wheeled their way towards you pushing a pram, then you were in real trouble. My other childhood memory of visits to the town was the strong pungent smell of the tannery, putting up a strong fight against the aroma of beer from the breweries. That strange and at times annoying mix of smells was enough to force anyone to run for the cover of a café or the next bus home for the fresh air of my village on top of the hill.

As noted, I returned to Wrexham permanently in 2010 having lived and worked in Swansea. I remember seeing an old friend of mine on the streets of the town. It being lunchtime I asked him, 'Where in Wrexham is a good place to eat?' He replied, 'Chester'.

At that time, if I looked down on Wrexham from the hill near my house, it struck me that the experience was not dissimilar to gazing into a giant concrete mouth. Nearly every time I looked, it seemed as if another tooth, or should I say building, was gone. Needless to say, the feel-good factor was missing.

Many young people wanted to move away and get jobs in cities such as Liverpool or Manchester, while the really adventurous opted for London. Those who were academically gifted would almost always take the escape routes offered by college or university. Such students would rarely return to live and work in the town of their birth.

When I was growing up in Rhos, the town and borough of Wrexham was somewhere where it was fairly easy to get a job. In addition to the Wrexham Industrial Estate, there were coal mines at Llay, Hafod, Gresford and Bersham. Often there was work to be found in the steelworks at either Brymbo or Shotton, too. Then, of course, one by one these centres of employment closed down and the slump slowly but surely turned Wrexham and its environs into a sad, post-industrial town with few prospects. I will never forget a young person telling me, 'We all know Wrexham is a bloody shithole, but at least it's my shithole.' A real sense of despair and hopelessness was evident, like a mist refusing to lift.

When I returned in 2010 it was not just the young people who gave the place the thumbs down. Talking with older inhabitants, they would tell me that Wrexham was nowhere near as good as it had been. They peppered me with details of boarded-up shops and other businesses which in their opinion would soon be gone. People were constantly looking over their shoulders at Chester and felt, by comparison, Wrexham was found wanting. As a returnee I was surprised. Of course there were problems and difficulties, but that was the case in most towns and cities in Britain, wasn't it?

As I looked around the town I felt it was on the up. Queen's Square had wonderful buildings, as did the old High Street with the impressive Wynnstay Arms Hotel keeping a watchful eye on the comings and goings of Wrexham inhabitants. As always, the locals were friendly, polite and chatty. From my personal point of view it could do with a theatre, while compared to Swansea it lacked a vibrant homespun culture or artistic community. I was glad to be back in the area and was loathe to knock it or condemn it as a no-hope place to live.

There were times when I felt that the local press did not help. There were a lot of good things happening in the area, yet the newspaper editors always seemed to choose lurid headlines for the front page. The two that stick in my mind are:

'MAN BITES EAR OF FELLOW DRINKER'
'SPICE ZOMBIES ON STREETS OF WREXHAM'

The second story was accompanied by a picture of a Spice addict completely 'out of it' lying on the street near Wrexham bus station. My main response when I first saw this headline was the hope that no one who was undecided about whether to move to Wrexham saw or read the reports.

I must admit that for the past few years the lead stories in the local paper have often portrayed Wrexham as a place where there is little going on except murders, drug trafficking, burglaries and public affray. In the past, heart-warming stories have been tucked away in the pages towards the back of the paper.

It's unfair to make it appear that only the local newspapers have been guilty of portraying the bad side of the town. A few years ago *Lonely Planet* published an article in which they listed 'Ten reasons not to visit Wrexham County this autumn'. The reasons were:

- Nothing for children to do in Wrexham
- No castles or history
- No adventure tourism
- Nowhere to fish
- No sailing

- Just sleepy boats floating along the Llangollen Canal
- You have to head to the mountain if you want off-road driving
- Nothing worth coming to Wrexham for
- All you can get is dirty kebab shops and cheap bars

It's only right that I point out that many people took to social media to challenge these views. It's also highly likely that if you're a reader who knows Wrexham, you have already been shouting your reasons for arguing with many points on the list.

At the end of the day, these headlines are based on perceptions. However, the sad fact is that perceptions stick in the mind for a long time, and can take an interminable age to be dislodged.

Of course, throughout my life the football club has been a place of joy for the town's inhabitants on many occasions. I, along with others, have known the unrivalled delight of promotions, FA Cup, League Cup and European Cup Winners' Cup exploits against famous teams. But now it was all doom and gloom. Every year newspapers and sports magazines, plus local radio stations, counted the years since we were in the English Football League. At the start of 2020–21 we were in our 13th season in non-league. The atmosphere inside the ground, even with 3,000 or 4,000 people there, was at times incredibly quiet and subdued. Sometimes I thought to myself there's probably a better and jollier atmosphere in a morgue. Even those who still watched them would tut-tut and shake their heads in disbelief if you mentioned Wrexham Football Club in a pub or a café. Then it all started to change. Along came Ryan Reynolds and Rob McElhenney.

WREXHAM, IMPROVING AS A PLACE

When I lived in Swansea I saw the phoenix-like rise of Swansea City Football Club from the fourth tier of the Football League to the giddy heights of the Premiership. I watched Swansea rejuvenate itself, and firms started reporting that if they had offices in the Welsh city many of their employees were asking to relocate there. Classy eating houses opened up and there was suddenly a buzz about the place, the like of which residents who had lived there for many years had never witnessed before.

In the two years since the Hollywood stars took over Wrexham FC, I would say that there has also been a resurgence in Wrexham. Firstly, after attempting to be called a city on two separate occasions and being pipped to the post, first by Newport then by Preston, Wrexham town eventually became Wrexham city in 2022. While the honour was bestowed by the Queen as part of her Platinum Jubilee celebrations, rather than by Rob and Ryan, one cannot help but wonder if the interest in the new city they engendered throughout Britain and abroad played some part in the decision. The new status went a long way to heal the hurt that the nearby tiny north Wales town of St Asaph had been granted city status before Wrexham.

After two years of Ryan and Rob's involvement with the city and the club, there is now a discernible difference in Wrexham people when you bump into them. Individuals, who a couple of years before would have moved to live elsewhere, are now content to stay put and watch the amazing story unfold. New eating places are sprouting up, such as the marvellous Levant, and we also have excellent wine bars such as The Bank.

In 2022 Wrexham reached the last six in their bid to become the 2025 City of Culture. Inspired by the close miss of losing out to Bradford, the council are bidding for it next time.

Not so many years ago, friends from other towns and cities would put on their disinterested face if I mentioned my love for Wrexham Football Club. Others would ask what league they were in, while there were some who assumed they played in the Welsh League. Many of them are now on the phone or contacting me by email to share the frequent news about Wrexham. I used to tell people that I had watched Wrexham through thin and thin rather than thick and thin! Since the takeover, it feels more like watching them through thick and thicker.

One of the aims expressed by Rob and Ryan when they took over the club was that they wanted to make Wrexham a global force. Many cynics guffawed when they heard that. As a town we'd struggled to get people from nearby places, such as Chester and Shrewsbury, to visit us or take us seriously. So how on earth were we ever going to have a global influence? Two years on from that bold aspiration, there are signs that it is starting to happen in a big way.

WREXHAM, A GLOBAL PRESENCE

Many years ago I was in an American bookshop with my daughter. We were approached by a smiling American. 'Where are you guys from? Is it Australia?' We bristled slightly and replied, 'Actually, we're from Wales.' Unabashed he said, 'Wales. Right. I know it. It's next to Sheffield, right?'

Before the revolution at the Racecourse Ground, the chances are that very few people in other countries had any idea where or what Wrexham was. That has all changed. Wrexham matches are now regularly screened by ESPN on American television.

In Australia, an ex-pupil of the grammar school I attended emailed to say Wrexham's spectacular FA Cup third round 3–4 victory in January 2023 over Championship side Coventry City was on Australian news. That game was also the first match on *Match of the Day*, while the fourth round tie against Championship side Sheffield United was screened live by the BBC and the replay was selected by ITV for live coverage. In the 2022–23 season it became obvious that it was not only in America or Canada that the team was making inroads, but countries as unexpected as Bhutan and Chad were now following the fortunes of Wrexham Football Club, too. In the early months, a group of Canadians flew over to watch a home game. This was no doubt due to Ryan Reynolds trumpeting the achievements of Wrexham in his native country.

On 18 October 2022 Wrexham were playing against Blyth Spartans in the FA Cup qualifying rounds and were leading, with just a few minutes to play, when Blyth managed to do the exact opposite of their previous Cup meeting and snatched a 1–1 draw. That game drew a small crowd of 2,787 spectators, but in America nearly a million watched it live on ESPN. Remarkably, the game was not even one of the proper rounds of the FA Cup. There can be no doubt that that TV audience has to be the biggest ever for a fourth qualifying round in the history of the FA Cup.

The global support for Wrexham has not just been via television. Individuals are now making long pilgrimages to Wrexham to get a taste of what is happening on the hallowed turf. The local paper reported that father and son, Ryan and Damon Hopkins, were spotted in the Turf pub, having travelled all the way from Australia to watch the Reds play Maidenhead. I had a personal experience in August 2022 of sitting in the lower Wrexham Lager Stand next to a woman who had come from Dubai to watch the match. I am pleased to say she was rewarded with a 3–1 victory over Gateshead.

Brian Lyck Jørgensen runs the Facebook page The Danish Reds, and has been following Wrexham since 1989. He arrived in Wrexham with his brother-in-law Bertram Bendicksen on 20 February 2023, a day before the Scunthorpe game. They were not to know, when making the long journey, that they had selected what was to be one of the most dire games of the season. Undaunted by the poor entertainment that was dished up that evening, Brian told the local paper that next time he wanted to come and stay for a few days so that he could take in a home match on a Tuesday and a Saturday. This will either mean that he sees two awful games or two scintillating matches! I know that the laws of mathematics and probabilities dictate there are other permutations. But this is Wrexham we're talking about. Since the documentary TV series, *Welcome to Wrexham*, Brian's Facebook site has been gaining more and more fans, and he claims that there are thousands of Danes who want to visit Wrexham.

SOCIAL MEDIA CASTS ITS NET AND PULLS IN MORE FANS

Gone are the not-so-distant days when BBC Radio Wales decided not to cover Wrexham FC matches. Apart from coverage on the local community radio station Calon FM, it was very difficult to follow Wrexham when they were playing away from home.

It's all very different now since Ryan and Rob took over. It's no exaggeration to say that Wrexham FC have become a powerhouse on social media. During the release of the *Welcome to Wrexham* series, there were one million Wrexham FC followers across the various social media sites. Inevitably, with the Reds now gracing screens in America on a regular basis through coverage of their games on ESPN, plus renewed interest in the club owing to their great exploits in the FA Cup against Championship sides Coventry City and Sheffield United, the number of followers on 13 February 2023 stood at 1.5 million.

In June 2021 Wrexham FC signed a two-year sponsorship deal with TikTok. With the company's name now emblazoned on the team-members' shirts, it has led to a greater following for Wrexham on TikTok. In February 2022 the club had 100,000 followers. A year later the figures had leapfrogged to a massive 660,000, with 6.5 million 'likes'.

In the 12 months to February 2023, the Twitter feed had gained 419.3 million views. This was an increase of more than 230 per cent over the 12-month period. In that same period Twitter numbers more than trebled, with 359,000 followers compared to 102,800 a year earlier.

Paul Mullin's amazing lob over the goalkeeper to gain the winner in stoppage time against Stockport in the FA Trophy semi-final in April 2022, was watched more than a million times. I was fortunate enough to be in the ground, and the sheer audacity of Mullin to even attempt a shot on goal took my breath away. The keeper ran out of his area and must have been very close to the touchline in front of the Macron Stand, about 30 metres away from his goal. I, along with many other fans, was expecting Mullin to try and dribble around the goalkeeper. Instead, he went for goal with one of the most glorious lobs I've ever seen. What a goal and what pictures of sheer joy in the opposite upper Wrexham Lager Stand where I was sitting. Ageing people like myself, who probably hadn't leapt into the air for a decade or more, were airborne for a very long time.

The club's full-time tweet at their home game against Dover on 26 March 2022 gained just over 16,000,000 views. Like the spectacular Mullin lob, I was lucky enough to be in the ground and see one of the most bizarre and incredible games I've ever witnessed. With 24 minutes left on the clock, Wrexham were in deep trouble. Their opponents, who had been relegated just a week before, were playing with the freedom and panache of a team who knew they had nothing to play for. All the pressure had been taken off them and they were 2–5 in front. I have to say that in the upper Wrexham Lager Stand the fans were streaming out, with many of them shouting 'rubbish' to their seated friends who had decided to stay to the bitter end. Then, everything was turned upside down. First, a third goal was scored by Wrexham, then the fourth, and then, unbelievably, a fifth. So from the jaws of despair we had snatched a point. But the Reds weren't finished yet, and in the final minutes Jordan Davies snatched the winner. A woman behind me thought that she was going to have a heart attack. She said that when the fourth goal entered the back of the Dover net. When Davies got the winner, I didn't have the courage to turn around and check if she was still with us! I wonder what those fans who left early felt like when they got into the town centre and heard that Wrexham were the 6–5 winners.

Those two games are not the only time that Wrexham FC have made it big on social media. In November 2022 Wrexham were in the top ten for views on the sports website FlashScore. Unbelievably, they were in the same company as footballing giants Liverpool, Manchester United, Barcelona and Real Madrid. Not bad for a team who are normally rubbing shoulders with the likes of Solihull Moors, Dagenham & Redbridge and Woking.

It's not just the crowds who are able to get into the Racecourse to watch matches who have palpitations watching the Reds!

MORE FANS

We have already seen how the crowds have been much bigger at the Racecourse since Ryan and Rob became co-owners. Of course, when they first took over in February 2021, as a nation we were still feeling the effects of Covid and lockdowns. Some of the games were played in empty stadia. But, even under Dean Keates' management, there were crowds of between 4,000 and 5,000 watching the home games. That all changed when Ryan and Rob experienced their first full season in charge of the club. As already noted, the average gate for the 2021–22 season was 8,647. In the next season there were regular crowds nudging the 10,000 mark.

At the beginning of the 2022–23 season there were many

fans, I have to say myself included, who wondered if there would be a drop in the number attending matches. After all, we had lost out to Grimsby Town in the play-offs at the end of the 2021–22 season, plus missed out in the FA Trophy at Wembley. There were some who felt downbeat and convinced we would never win anything. They were the 'here we go again, same as before' brigade.

Such people would have been as amazed, as I was, that in the close season the club sold 7,000 season tickets. That was 2,000 to 3,000 more than were watching us in previous seasons. I also remember being in the club shop in the early days of the 2021–22 season to buy a ticket for the home match against Dagenham & Redbridge. Someone announced that if anyone was after an away ticket for the game at Edgeley Park against Stockport County, unfortunately there were none left. The club had sold their entire allocation of 1,700 tickets for Wrexham fans in an hour!

It was a similar story in the 2022–23 season, with the away fans often topping the 1,000 mark. At some of the smaller grounds there would be as many Wrexham supporters (or sometimes even more) as home fans. This was all the more impressive when you realise the distances that the team and their followers had to travel in that season. Within the league only four teams, Oldham Athletic, Altrincham, York City and Halifax Town, could be considered 'northern clubs'. York City's ground still represents a long haul. All of the rest represent huge treks down south. The list below shows the long distances the team and fans have to travel to some of their away games. The mileage is based on round trips.

Torquay United: 486
Maidstone: 508
Southend: 430
Yeovil: 406

Eastleigh: 408
Dorking: 410
Aldershot: 406
Dagenham: 404
Woking: 384
Gateshead: 386
Scunthorpe: 284
York City: 248
TOTAL: 5,008 miles

This particular season was also noteworthy for the crowds following Wrexham in the two big FA Cup matches, with over 4,000 watching the spectacular 3–4 away victory over Championship side Coventry City, and another large away crowd watching the replay at Bramall Lane against Sheffield United, which we sadly lost 3–1.

MONEY PILES IN, MERCHANDISE FLIES OUT

Since the release of the *Welcome to Wrexham* docu-series, the club reported that they had made £360,000 on merchandise sales alone. So many people from all around the world seemed anxious to buy whatever items they could bearing Wrexham's name and crest. Even Ryan Reynolds bemoaned the fact that he was struggling to get a shirt! Before Christmas 2022, the club shop received a delivery of 5,100 home and away shirts. They decided to sell them at a retail price of £37.50. They also stipulated that no more would be available once that stock had been sold. In addition, fans were only allowed to buy one item. While these measures were introduced in response to massive demand, there was also the fear that rogue dealers were flooding the market with fake merchandise.

KOP A LOAD OF THIS

When we think of the influence the new owners have had on our once sad and dispirited club, we realise it's not just at present that things are looking good, but also so are future plans. Nowhere is this more evident than when they share their ideas about the now defunct Kop. This large terraced stand, behind one of the goals, which for decades was standing-room only, was closed in 2008 and declared unsafe for fans.

As a youngster I sometimes stood on the huge plinth where one of the floodlights stood. It gave me a better view of what was going on on the pitch. In my early twenties I stood and watched on the Kop terraces. These were the halcyon days of the Seventies, and it was from here I watched and cheered Wrexham on for their great FA Cup, League Cup, European Cup Winners' Cup matches before their exploits culminated in them winning the Third Division championship to enter the Second Division for the first and only time in their history. I would often stand towards the back of the Kop, and I could see the team in full flight as the skills of Mel Sutton, Les Cartwright, Dixie McNeil, Billy Ashcroft and the rest helped the boys in red swoop past their opponents with ease. It was like watching chess players on Speed, looking for the gap, going for the kill. All these years on, I still have those exciting images in my mind.

Sometimes, of course, I couldn't get to the back of the Kop, so I would try and find somewhere near the middle. If Wrexham scored, the crowd would push forwards in sheer joy to be as close to their heroes as they could. The players would also stand as near to the barriers as possible. They would milk the adulation until the referee intervened and told them to get back to the halfway line to restart the game.

When the crowd at the back pushed down like that, it felt to me as if there was a mountain on my back. When I was young and considerably smaller than the six footer I am now, I would find myself lifted off the terrace, with people almost lying on top of me, just as I was on top of the fans in front of me. It was a strange sensation, and for a minute or so you began to wonder whether you would ever find the spot you were standing on, or whether you would have to watch the rest of the game in this weird and uncomfortable state. Eventually, the crowd controllers at the back of the Kop would return to where they had started the crush. This ensured that normal standing positions resumed.

In the late Seventies, when Wrexham won the Third Division championship and did so well in the Cups, attendances at the ground were sometimes in the region of 18,000. Towards the end of the season they would top the 20,000 mark. This, of course, was in the days before all-seater stadia. In that period the Racecourse was also used for international matches, and I was privileged to stand on the Kop for a match between Wales and Czechoslovakia in 1977. The opposition had won the UEFA European Football Championship the previous year. This was long before Wales became a strong force in international football. Everyone was expecting a thrashing from this talented group of stars. Amazingly, Wales turned on a wonderful performance and won 3–0. I was 18, and it was in the days of slip-on shoes. At the final whistle I made my way down the bank behind the Kop onto Crispin Lane. As I hit the Mold Road, the Kop crowd was joined by hundreds if not thousands from the Mold Road end of the ground. It wasn't so much that I was in trouble, it's more accurate to say that my shoes were struggling. One of my slip-ons came off. I now had a huge decision to make about the force of the crowd behind me and the momentum of the thousands in front of me. Should I turn around and see if I could retrieve my shoe? Mercifully, what little common sense I had at that age kicked in and, rather than go on all fours for the missing shoe and get crushed to death, I hobbled on. Eventually, the crowd thinned out a little as we neared the town.

One of the hopes that Rob and Ryan had from the beginning was that the old Kop would be pulled down and a new modern stand would take its place. In the autumn of 2022 Wrexham passed plans for the work to go ahead. While sitting in the ground for the 2023 matches, it's been obvious that the work has started. At the time of writing, the Kop is now demolished and countless lorries have removed the rubble. But it's not all rosy and full steam ahead. Although Wrexham County Borough Council managed to gain £25million from the Welsh Government for the project, the council announced that they had been unsuccessful in their bid for financial support for the redevelopment of the Kop. If the council had succeeded, the money would have covered groundworks for a hotel, conference facilities and car parking. It's to be hoped that ambitions to build a stand that will accommodate 5,500 people and also make the stadium capable of housing more international matches will come to fruition.

MANY OTHER BENEFITS

In this section I've concentrated on just some of the effects Rob and Ryan have had on the club and the city. Not many clubs can say that the King and Queen have already been to their stadium. Charles and Camilla paid a visit when they attended a service at St Giles parish church to commemorate Wrexham being given city status.

As well as the increase in attendance and revenue at the club, Rob and Ryan's financial input has also meant that Phil Parkinson has been able to draft in top players. Almost all of those he has signed have played in the Championship. It's for this reason that Wrexham has looked far better than most of the other teams in their league in the last two seasons.

Rob and Ryan's investment has also meant that facilities have improved, such as a new gym. The two have also supported Kerry Evans, the disability officer, and that particular aspect has become more prominent.

CHAPTER II

THE 2022-23 SEASON

SUMMER BREAK WOBBLES

WHILE THE FOOTBALL management team spent the summer break recruiting brilliant players, I spent most of it worrying on behalf of Wrexham Football Club. Yes, we had experienced the first full season with Rob and Ryan in charge of the club, and I had to admit it had been a great season with wonderful games and fantastic crowds. Before you start wondering if I'm one of those unrealistic fans who expected us to gain promotion in the Hollywood stars' first full season, I assure you I'm not. I was not fuelled by dreams of the club seamlessly moving through two divisions of the English Football League, then the Championship, until they sat in an uncatchable position on top of the Premier League in early May 2027. The fact that the first element of those unrealistic hopes had not been achieved made no contribution to my state of anxiety. Why, then, was I in the doldrums before the kick-off the new 2022–23 season?

I suppose it was all to do with the fact that, despite some great football at times and some amazing new signings in the previous season – Ollie Palmer, Paul Mullin and Ben Tozer, plus his towel which in many games had been our 12th man – we still had to face reality. We were still a fifth-tier side, who for the fourth time during our stay in the National League had failed at the play-off stage. Were we doomed to live out this scenario for ever? Was it that Wrexham were the perennial close-run failures of non-league football, falling at the final hurdle in every title race?

I was also wondering whether those crowds of 8,000+ (sometimes 9,000+) would keep the faith. Would the extra 4,000 to 5,000 we had picked up in that 2021–22 season go back to what they used to do on a Saturday afternoon and some Tuesday evenings?

When getting tickets for the first game I could go to, I stood in the queue and realised that my fears – about missing out on promotion the previous season affecting our support for the new season – were ill-founded. Chatting with fellow fans I discovered that, as noted already, over 7,000 people had bought season tickets. My only hope was to become a member and get tickets for the home matches.

AUGUST

The National Trust are to blame for me missing the opening match of the season, at home to Eastleigh. They are a team remembered by Wrexham fans for all the wrong reasons. When Bryan Hughes was manager, we made the play-offs and were pitted against the Hampshire club. Wrexham gave a great performance and dominated the game. Their keeper made some great saves, and as always we missed some good chances, but their keeper also was ultimately to become the villain of the piece. He perfected the art of going down in his penalty area and making it look like he'd been fouled. Like so many referees in this lowly division, the official gave him the benefit of the doubt. Then, out of nowhere, one of their players scored a worldie. It was their only shot on target that I can recall, but you must remember I'm a fan rather than a football commentator. Needless to say, at the final whistle we were out of the play-offs, with another season in the Vanarama National League beckoning.

SQUIRE YORKE WON'T LET ME GO TO THE FOOTBALL

As already mentioned, the responsibility for me missing the big kick-off in 2022 lies at the door of the National Trust. Since 2017 I've been commissioned to write a play for Erddig Hall which is performed throughout July, August and early September. So rather than shouting the boys on to victory, I had to be content with getting snatches of the score and updates from Wrexham fans who were in the grounds of Erddig Hall. Needless to say, such people were few and far between. I should have thought the situation through, and would have quickly realised that the only reason most of these people were at Erddig was because they had little or no interest in the beautiful game.

I have played Squire Philip Scott Yorke, the last squire of Erddig, many times in my one-man shows. People tell me that I bear a striking resemblance to him, and the first time I did a one-man show about him I ended up in a spot of bother. It was the 40th anniversary of the opening of Erddig to the public after massive renovations and work on the stunning gardens. Having given my all in my 45-minute one-man show, I realised that I had a couple of hours respite before the next performance. I decided to saunter around the grounds and relax. I soon heard a very irate voice shouting loudly, 'Excuse me, can I have a word with you?' I turned around to see a teacher with children in tow. 'I have just taken my pupils around the house and have spent the last hour convincing them that Philip Yorke died in 1978. They came out and a couple of them screamed when they saw you, and another is convinced he's seen a ghost.'

THE REDS' AUGUST FORM

From all the reports, there wasn't much excitement in the Eastleigh match, which Wrexham won rather unconvincingly,

2–1. This was followed by a 1–1 draw at Yeovil. Then the Reds were away at Chesterfield. Most ardent followers of non-league football were convinced that the teams vying for top spot that season would be Wrexham, Notts County and Chesterfield. For this match, the Derbyshire club welcomed a bumper crowd of 8,057, at least 2,000 of whom were from Wrexham. The 2–0 scoreline in favour of the home side meant that in their first three games Wrexham had gained just four points out of a possible nine. The football sages who walk the streets of Wrexham or populate the bars, or do both, were already blowing sirens of despair.

'Knew this was going to happen', 'Same as before, dreadful', 'We're going to miss out again'. I was not so pessimistic. After all, we had only played three games and had another 43 to go. It was surely too early to do the football fans' utter despair act. Of course, if I said this to my football friends they would reply, 'What do you know? You haven't seen them yet, have you?' I had every intention of righting that situation the following Saturday. Wrexham were at home to Maidstone United. Surely this would be the game where Wrexham would turn the corner and put their promotion challenge back on track. I looked in my diary to check that it was a 3pm kick-off and not a 5.30pm BT Sport match. It was quite a few minutes before I stopped standing like a frozen statue clutching an open diary. It was also the 50th birthday of my very good friend Aaron Neal. He wanted guests to arrive at 3pm at his house.

So the following Saturday I enjoyed a wonderful party at Aaron's. Honestly! It was a lovely afternoon which meant that all the guests sat outside. Wonderful wine, wonderful food. As the crow flies, Aaron's house is not far from the Racecourse. This meant we could hear the roar every time Wrexham scored. A huge roar. One goal for Wrexham. This occurred another four times. In pre-social media days you would know that Wrexham had scored five times, but it was only when you got home to check with the television or radio that you knew how many their opponents had put in the back of Wrexham's net. Mercifully, Wrexham won 5–0 and that was confirmed by three or four guests who arrived late because they'd been to the match. I must repeat that it was a great party and Aaron is still a very good friend. But I must confess, following a match in that audio style is a little like being outside a locked arena where your favourite band or singer is performing, and you have no chance of seeing them, only hearing blurred snatches from their numbers.

Although I missed the game, I drove home from the party happy that Wrexham had at least managed a comprehensive victory. Once at home I was able to check the scorers and was delighted to see that our dynamic striker, Paul Mullin, had got a hat trick, with one goal coming from Jordan Davies, plus an own goal. The Maidstone victory certainly turned out to be the spark that ignited Wrexham's season. After that game they embarked on an unbeaten run of seven games. Six were victories, with one goalless draw at Roots Hall against Southend United. The run makes impressive reading: Woking, away, 2–3; Gateshead, home, 3–1; Dorking Wanderers, away, 0–5; Dagenham & Redbridge, home, 4–1; Torquay United, home, 6–0; Oldham Athletic, away, 1–2. It was after that victory that we suffered our second defeat of the season.

GATESHEAD IN TOWN

The first game I saw in the 2022–23 season was the home encounter against Gateshead. I must confess I have always had a soft spot for the visitors. When I started watching Wrexham as a boy, just a few seasons earlier, Gateshead had finished in the bottom four of the Fourth Division. They failed to secure reselection (which is how it worked in those days) and were replaced by Peterborough United. My father was born in the Newcastle area and he used to tell me tales of the great forward, Hughie Gallacher, who played for Newcastle United in the then First Division, before ending his career at Gateshead. Sadly, the drop from top-flight football to the basement was something Gallacher couldn't take, and he tragically took his own life. When I was a boy my father used do shimmies in the kitchen. His 50-year-old limbs showed me how Gallacher trapped the ball, then left the opposing defender on the ground, before rocketing the ball into the top corner. As I made my way to the ground for Wrexham's home match with Gateshead, I realised why I still wanted them to do well (with the exception of that night). It also brought smiles to my face as I thought of my father. The happiness the memories brought was tinged with disappointment, as I remembered that when I was young he was no longer interested in football, meaning I had to find others to take me to matches.

So there I was for my first sighting of Wrexham in the 2022–23 season. Of course the first thing I saw were the floodlights. Whenever I see them I am like a human moth. As an adult, when I had a travelling job, if I saw floodlights on in a town or city I would follow the light, park my car, and if there was still time before kick-off make my way to the turnstiles to pay and watch the match. This has resulted in me watching random teams in stadia as diverse as Stoke City, Aberdeen and Rossendale United.

After a break of three months from watching live football, I was determined to soak in the atmosphere. Although I was on the Mold Road heading to the ground a good 30 minutes before the game, it was obvious from the droves of supporters behind and ahead of me that Wrexham were heading for another bumper crowd, probably well in excess of 9,000. It was great to see people wearing red Wrexham shirts with no hint of a Premiership shirt anywhere. Also, as I indulged in my favourite hobby of eavesdropping, it was a joy to realise that individuals were talking to their friends about

Wrexham's players and performances. This was so different to a few years ago when many of Wrexham's matches weren't probably worth talking about. Instead, people would share details of matches they'd seen at Anfield, Goodison Park, Old Trafford, the Etihad Stadium, or a cracking match involving top teams recently seen on Sky Sports. What a change Rob and Ryan, along with Phil Parkinson the backroom staff and, of course, the players had made to the atmosphere and optimism among the supporters.

Once inside the ground I sat back in my seat and soaked it all in. It's amazing that I was sitting outside in the open air on a cold, autumn evening. I would never contemplate sitting out in my garden in the evening at this time of year. No longer able to rely on my friend's season ticket, I was at the mercy of the membership system and relied on getting to the club shop early on the day that their website told me tickets were available. Unlike the previous season it meant that, unless I was very lucky, I would be sitting in a different seat for each match. Tonight I was in the front row of the lower Wrexham Lager Stand. I'd sat in this area a few times in the early days of the previous season, before negotiating with my friend to buy his season ticket off him game by game. It's so different to watching the match high up in the stands. Up there you are looking at silent, moving sportsmen. Down here you almost feel as if you are taking part in the game yourself. You hear the grunts and screams as crunching tackles hit the mark. The sweat on the players' foreheads and shirts is visible. I now understand why fans sitting near the front of a stand get so involved in shouting directions to players and officials. It's important you resist the temptation to climb over the hoarding and give them a hand. Players are running towards or right near you, and sometimes you may have a chance, if the ball is heading directly for you, to catch or head it back to the field of play. Thankfully, I've never been in that position, or else if I'd tried to do either my ageing body would have caused deafening laughter rather than applause from the crowd around me.

Applause is given throughout the match by a crowd just 200 short of 10,000. It rises to tumultuous levels as the players leave at the end, with goals by Tozer, Palmer and Mullin in their 3–1 victory.

SEPTEMBER

In their next game, away to Dorking, the emphasis seems to be on the owner of the newly-promoted club rather than on the Wrexham players. Marc White is the owner, chairman and team manger of the Wanderers. In 23 years at the helm, he has overseen no less than 12 promotions. In that time the Surrey club, which started life playing in Sunday Park League games, has risen to the top echelons of non-league football, and the 2022–23 season marked their first one in the Vanarama National League. It's a remarkable story, one that became even more incredible for some of the many Wrexham fans who had crammed their way into a pub near Dorking's ground. Marc White was so impressed by the number of supporters who had made the long trip from Wales that he entered the drinking den and told the barman to open a tab for the visiting fans. He obviously realised that the 2,730 crowd that day would consist of over 1,000 Wrexham fans.

Happy to hand over the money to the barman, he expressed his thanks and admiration for the large number of Welsh visitors. At five o'clock he was clearly not so happy. Wrexham eventually coasted to a 0–5 victory, with Palmer scoring twice, plus one each from Lee and Mendy, and an own goal by Moore. Marc White gave a post-match interview to local sports media which was full of foul-mouthed expletives. Needless to say, the interview went viral with thousands of hits.

It would be interesting to know whether the 0–5 drubbing

he'd watched his boys endure made him rethink comments he'd made in the past about his attitude to potential investors buying into his club. As far as he was concerned, he was not open to any such interference. It was his belief that there was such a winning mentality among his staff and players that they could cope and keep rising up the leagues without help from anyone. Despite those comments, I still wonder if seeing the effects of Rob and Ryan's ownership on Wrexham left Marc White having second thoughts as he quaffed his post-match drink.

On Tuesday, 13 September, I turned up at the Racecourse and took my seat with some trepidation. The visitors were Dagenham & Redbridge who boasted a good record of victories over us in previous seasons. Although we had won four consecutive matches since losing to Chesterfield, this was Wrexham we were talking about. As it turned out, it was easier than I anticipated and we beat them quite comfortably, the four goals in our 4–1 victory coming from our two main strikers, Mullin and Palmer, who bagged a brace each. This was followed by a 0–0 draw away to Southend, as already mentioned.

TORQUAY UNITED

In the 2021–22 season the home game against Torquay had been memorable for the fact that it was the first time Ryan and Rob had got to see Wrexham at the Racecourse. In the 2022–23 season both teams again played in the autumn. In Gary Johnson, the West Country team had a very experienced, successful manager. When they arrived at Wrexham for this game on 24 September, they were in some trouble towards the bottom of the table. For the first 20 minutes or so they made a fist of it, and looked as if they were holding their own. Slowly but surely Wrexham got on top, and at half-time were in the lead having scored three goals without reply. In the second half things got much better for the home team, and much, much worse for the visitors. Wrexham scored another three, and towards the end of the match Wrexham were leading 6–0. I was in the upper Wrexham Lager Stand and made my way down to the lower part as I was due at a dinner of the old boys of Ruabon Grammar School and needed to leave the house at six o'clock. I stood near the corner flag knowing that when the final whistle went, I would be able to make a quick getaway. Standing next to me was someone who turned out be the father of Jordan Tunnicliffe's girlfriend. Tunnicliffe had signed for the club, but up to that point had not been able to break into the team. Jordan had decided to come to Wrexham, despite the fact that he knew there were some fine players ahead of him at the club. Wrexham, though, were offering him far more than he got from League One Crawley Town. So he decided to move to the north Wales club and try and push his way into the squad. This is exactly what he has done, and despite a couple of injuries in the second half of the 2022–23 season, he has been a dominant presence in defence for the team.

OCTOBER

On 1 October our away fans helped to swell Oldham Athletic's attendance to 9,496. David Unsworth had left Everton to take control at Boundary Park. While Notts County, now in the Vanarama National League, had once been a First Division side in the English League, the dubious honour of being the first club to have played in the Premiership, prior to sliding down all the divisions before landing in the Vanarama National League, belonged to Oldham who, along with Scunthorpe United (a second-tier side not all that long ago), were relegated to the fifth tier. It was David Unsworth's first game in charge, and by half-time it looked as if the 'bounce' principle – which new men in the dugout often bring to their club – was going to work for the 'Latics as, at half-time, Oldham led 1–0. Fortunately for Wrexham this was not to be the case, as in the second half Tozer and Mullin were the scorers in a 1–2 victory.

Unfortunately, there was crowd trouble before the game as Oldham and Wrexham fans clashed in the streets near the ground. There were stories of terrified passengers trapped in their cars as the fighting raged around their vehicles. There were arrests by the police and subsequent court appearances for fans who were banned for life from their respective clubs. After that match at Boundary Park, some of my friends, who like me are older, expressed concern that if Wrexham progressed up the leagues in future seasons, as we all hoped they would, there was the possibility that crowds would be larger, especially once the Kop stand was rebuilt, and there could be the possibility of more crowd violence. Fingers crossed that this will not happen. As far as I am aware, there was only one incident at Wrexham in the 2021–22 season, before and after the FA Trophy semi-final match. As I came out of Crispin Road to walk into town, a policeman stopped me. 'I'm 71 with osteoarthritis in both knees and serious heart problems. I'm not planning on causing any trouble.' I'm glad to say he waved me through and I went for a drink in the town.

The next game was away at Notts County on Tuesday, 4 October. Although Wrexham played well and put up a good fight, the home side ran out as 1–0 winners. For the next few days the harbingers of doom were out in force once more. Although after 12 games we had only been beaten twice, they pointed out that we had lost to the two teams who posed the biggest threat to us in claiming automatic promotion. However, I'd seen enough excellent football to suggest we were good enough to gain automatic promotion, although Notts County were arguably the biggest threat.

THE BARNET BONANZA

The next game at home on 8 October was one that those who were lucky enough to see it will never forget. Barnet, who at the start of the season had been many people's favourites to struggle if not get relegated, had pulled themselves together with some good results. By the time they arrived at the Racecourse they were hovering around the play-off places in 11th position.

It was 3–2 to Wrexham at half-time and I would guess that very few of the 9,987 crowd were expecting another five goals in the second half. As it turned out they were correct. Sitting in the lower Wrexham Lager Stand, my neighbours turned out to be the financial officer of the club, plus his family and friends. We, along with everyone else, sat with our mouths wide open in disbelief. I did tell you that the last 45 minutes did not provide another five goals. Instead we watched the ball hit the back of nets on seven occasions! That's right, seven goals. The head of finance turned to me at one point and said, 'Every time one of the teams moves forward, it looks like they'll score.' It really was one of those games. The season before we had been fortunate to see an 11-goal thriller against Dover, which Wrexham won 6–5. That game had equalled the record for the most goals scored at the Racecourse in a professional match (10–1 to Wrexham v Hartlepool).

What we witnessed that afternoon was a new record as Wrexham ran out 7–5 winners in front of a rather disbelieving crowd. Needless to say, both defences had bad days at the office, while all the attack-minded players had games they'll never forget. Hayden and Mullin scored two apiece, while Palmer, O'Connor and Young bagged a goal each. I should also mention that one of Paul Mullin's was from a penalty. Even as I write that fact, I am suddenly transported back to the Racecourse where I can see Mullin running to the penalty spot, then thrashing the ball down the throat of the goalkeeper. For those not familiar with football jargon and/ or anxious about Health and Safety issues, I should point out that 'thrashing the ball down the throat of the goalkeeper' is a metaphor, not an actual fact. Perhaps I should also add that no one was hurt or killed scoring the goal.

BLYTH SPIRIT

The following week Wrexham were in action at Blyth Spartans in the fourth qualifying round of the FA Cup. Of course, as a club, Wrexham have previous with Blyth. In the late Seventies, which was the previous golden era for the club, we played them in the fifth round of the FA Cup. I watched that match from the Kop. Blyth took an early lead which they held on to right until the dying moments of the game. Then, trailing 0–1, and facing a massive FA Cup embarrassment, Wrexham were awarded a corner. The ball was sent over, and Dixie McNeil scored the last-gasp equaliser to earn a replay in the north-east. There was so much interest in the replay that Blyth gave up their home advantage and played at St James' Park, Newcastle. The estimates regarding the attendance vary depending on who is writing, but I believe it was over 50,000, which is pretty impressive for a match between a non-league club and a team from the third tier of the Football League. (Wrexham won the replay and progressed into the quarter-finals where they were beaten 2–3 by Arsenal, a game I was also fortunate enough to be at.) Given that the attendance for the Blyth match at the Racecourse was just over 18,000, the two matches attracted just over 70,000. Incredible.

It's only fair to stress that after that 1978 game against Blyth there was huge controversy over Wrexham's equaliser which came from the corner kick and Dixie McNeil's header. The Blyth players and fans were convinced that the ball was not placed on the small circle for corner kicks. As far as they were concerned the goal should not have been allowed and the corner should have been retaken. If that had happened, who knows what the result would have been. More than likely, Blyth would have won. Everyone connected with the north-east club is still aggrieved about that match. So aggrieved that one of their fans wrote a book about the match and its perceived miscarriage of justice at the Racecourse.

Needless to say, the tie in 2022 did not appeal to such large physical crowds although, as noted, it was covered by ESPN in the United States and watched by nearly a million viewers. Wrexham drew 1–1 away, and won the replay 3–2.

FANCY SITTING NEXT TO YOU

In the next league game Wrexham drew 1–1 away to Boreham Wood. Their next home league encounter was with Halifax. Once again I was in the lower Wrexham Lager Stand and it's quite amazing who you meet at football matches. The gentleman sitting next to me, from Prestatyn, was a head teacher at the primary school in Saltney near Chester. Having to make such long trips every day to Saltney, and the modern demands on head teachers, he had very little time to get to matches. I discovered that his daughter worked for the Welsh Books Council and had been responsible for the grant to the publisher who was commissioning a book about Wrexham from a writer. The writer was of course me! What a small world we all live in!

Wrexham's second-half performance was far stronger than the first, and after going off 0–1 down at half-time they rallied to beat Halifax, 3–1. The next two matches were both won by Wrexham. This meant that after 14 league games, Wrexham were in second place in the table, just three points behind Notts County. The pattern was definitely set and things were to stay this way for the majority of the season.

Fans in the stands were often concentrating on two matches at the same time. They were mainly concerned about what was happening on the pitch, but mobile phones were also constantly consulted to find out whether Notts County were winning. Notts County would often be drawing, while Wrexham were winning, meaning that Wrexham could leapfrog them to top spot either on goal difference or sometimes by just one point. The holder of the mobile phone would announce the score to someone nearby and this would be passed down the rows. Again and again, annoyingly, Notts County would snatch a winner at the death, meaning that at the final whistle they would still be in pole position. Wrexham defeated Altrincham, 4–0, in late October.

NOVEMBER

The new month heralded a 1–0 home victory for Wrexham against Maidenhead, the goal scored by Aaron Hayden. It's worth mentioning that, although a defender, he scored many goals for Wrexham as part of a three-pronged group. This group also consisted of Tozer's towel, which he used before hurling his 'throw-in' into the penalty area in the hope that one of his team-mates would get a header on target. That team-mate was often Aaron Hayden. Tozer had also made a name for himself and his towel when playing at Newport County. I always enjoyed watching him sit on the hoarding, with wiped ball in his hands, before propelling himself forward with a big launch as the ball flew through the air. So the trinity of towel, Tozer and Hayden bagged many goals between them.

It was interesting to realise that as the season wore on more and more clubs got wise to the towel situation. Eventually, it became obvious that when Wrexham were playing away from home their opponents would make sure that there was no towel available for the Tozer throw. Not to be outdone by the hosts' unhelpfulness, Wrexham fans rallied to the cause. Some of them took a towel with them to away games and handed it to Ben Tozer if he needed it!

Next up were Oldham Athletic at the Racecourse, meaning that this FA Cup tie was the fourth home game on the trot. Wrexham easily dispatched their opponents 3–0 in front of the BBC cameras. Oldham's owner had done himself no favours ahead of the game by pouring scorn on Wrexham as a team. He also committed the unforgivable sin of saying that he had no idea who Ryan Reynolds or Rob McElhenney were, as he had never heard of them. If you weren't at the match, you will be able to guess what kind of welcome he received from the Wrexham faithful.

˙WE ARE TOP OF THE LEAGUE˙

That was the chant at the end of the next league game, away to Scunthorpe United. It was also the headline on the local paper's back page the following evening. Wrexham were victorious, scoring three goals to Scunthorpe's one. Scunny, as they are affectionately known by their fans, were having a wretched season in the Vanarama National League. They were relegated to the fifth tier, along with Oldham Athletic, at the end of the 2021–22 season. For seven of the ten seasons before their demise, they had been in League One, finishing seventh in 2015–16, third in the 2016–17 season, and fifth the following season, 2017–18. At the end of the 2022–23 season they were relegated from the Vanarama National League too, having spent most of the season in the doldrums. Amazingly, all four teams relegated had at one time been in the English Football League. Scunthorpe United, Maidstone United, Yeovil Town and Torquay United had all enjoyed seasons in the heady heights of the English Football League. This fact alone is proof enough of what a tortuous journey it is to get out of the National League. Perhaps, more to the point, it's also proof of how easy it is to slide down the slippery slope into soccer oblivion.

DECEMBER

The month began with an away match at York City. The home team were finding life in the Vanarama National League extremely difficult. For everyone connected with the Yorkshire club, they were far too near the drop zone. Wrexham turned out in force for the away trip. York's position, the fact that this was their new manager's first game in charge, and the number of away fans, all contributed to a bumper crowd of 7,145. The home team went ahead but, mercifully, in the second half O'Connor equalised to give Wrexham a point.

The following week saw a better away performance, with Wrexham triumphing at Eastleigh, the goals coming from Tozer and Lee. After that, Wrexham were in action in the FA Trophy against Scunthorpe which was won 3–1, despite the away team making a fight of it having been level at 1–1 at half-time.

So many fans had mixed feelings about progressing in this particular Cup. After all, they argued, the pressure of trying to win promotion and the FA Trophy at Wembley at the end of the previous season had resulted in us ending the season empty-handed. The month was rounded off with a resounding 5–0 home victory over our old rivals Solihull Moors, who normally drew or beat us. Paul Mullin scored a hat trick, with the other goals coming from Palmer and Hayden.

Pundits will always tell you that you shouldn't really look at the league tables until Christmas. Only then will they give you an inkling of how you are doing and how the season may turn out at the end of May. Of course, such a view is just that and not a fact. Even so, everyone connected to the club had every right to feel confident at the halfway stage. Wrexham had lost only one of their last 20 games, which was the 1–0 defeat away to Notts County. With still many games to go, it was already starting to look as if the battle for the top spot would be between Notts County and Wrexham.

JANUARY

After thrashing Solihull at the Racecourse, the away holiday fixture at their Damson Parkway stadium was much more tightly contested, with Wrexham triumphing, 1–2. The next game was an appetising FA Cup third round tie away to Championship side Coventry City. I sadly missed the game 'in the flesh', and it turned out to be an absolute cracker. Wrexham started the game like a Premiership side and Dalby got the ball rolling with a beautifully-headed goal. By half-time we were 1–3 up. Everyone in the TV studio was gasping in disbelief. What on earth was going on? Coventry are a good Championship side aren't they, and Wrexham are a non-league outfit, aren't they? In the second half, with Wrexham now in control at 1–4, the Coventry manager made substitutions and brought on some of his top players. Soon, Coventry went down to ten men after a sending off and I just feared that the home side would rally and try and make a match of it. The players had been booed off at half-time and the manager was to say in his post-match analysis that Coventry's performance had been embarrassing. The feared rally certainly arrived and, with just a few minutes left, Wrexham were hanging on to a 3–4 lead. At last the final whistle was blown and Wrexham had yet another famous Cup scalp to add to their collection. The following Monday most Wrexham fans watched us being drawn out of the hat for a home match against Sheffield United, who at that point were second in the Championship.

There was a slight feel of 'after the Lord Mayor's party' after that sterling performance and result in the FA Cup. In the Bromley match at the Racecourse on the following Tuesday night, the players looked jaded, tired and out of sorts. They made heavy weather of defeating Bromley 2–1 through a Mullin penalty and a goal by James Jones. Three days later they were away at Altrincham in the FA Trophy. Leading 1–2 in the dying moments, they surrendered their lead and the game went to penalties, which Wrexham lost. Not too many tears were shed by the faithful fans. It now meant that they could concentrate on the league, though there was, of course, still a possibility of more FA Cup glory.

There were two more league games in quick succession, Maidstone away, which ended 2–3 in Wrexham's favour, and then a long trek to Gateshead the following Tuesday. Well over 600 fans made the journey, and that meant that the Wrexham contingent made up nearly half of the 1,422 crowd. O'Connor, Palmer and Mullin rewarded the fans by scoring the goals in a 0–3 victory.

Next up was the eagerly anticipated home match in the FA Cup against Sheffield United. The game, which was live on the BBC, got off to the worst possible start with Wrexham conceding in the opening minutes. McBurnie scored for the opposition, a player well known to Wrexham as he used to play for Chester. So 0–1 down after two minutes was not what Wrexham fans wanted. If they were feeling down at that point, then their mood got darker after a further eight minutes. By then, two of our players, Hayden and Tunnicliffe, had been carried off with bad injuries. The fear among Wrexham fans was that, by half-time, United could have been too far ahead to catch. So it was with some relief that fans heard the half-time whistle, trailing by only one goal.

In the second half Wrexham came out fighting, and after five minutes were back on level terms through a James Jones goal. Eleven minutes later Wrexham were now delirious, as Thomas O'Connor scored to make it 2–1 to Wrexham. However, we only had four minutes to celebrate, as in the 65th minute Oliver Norwood levelled the scores.

In the 71st minute, Sheffield's Daniel Jebbison was sent off. Then in the 86th minute, Paul Mullin scored to put the home team 3–2 ahead with just four minutes of normal time remaining. Surely we could hold out against the ten men. But, in the fifth minute of added-on time, with fans in various parts of the world, as well as those at the Racecourse screaming at the referee to blow his whistle, John Egan equalised for the Blades. All square, 3–3.

FEBRUARY

After that epic tussle against Sheffield United, Wrexham beat Altrincham away 1–2. Three days later, the team were off to Bramall Lane for the FA Cup fourth round replay. The Wrexham players certainly gave as good as they got, and at half-time, with the game goalless, there was the slight whiff of an upset in the air. But then Sheffield United's Ahmedhodžić put the home team ahead in the 50th minute. Paul Mullin scored from the penalty spot, but also missed a penalty. With scores level at 1–1, the match went into added-on time. Wrexham pushed forward but they were caught out by the speed of the home attackers and Billy Sharp and Sander Berge added two goals to give Sheffield United a 3–1 win. I think the way Wrexham played in those two games and against Coventry must have won them many more admirers.

In some February games there was often a strange mix of tension and caution. Since Rob and Ryan's first full season in charge, there had been a swagger and confidence in the way Wrexham played. That had certainly been the case in the amazing 7–5 result against Barnet, the 6–0 victory over Torquay, 3–4 at Coventry and 0–5 away to Dorking. I'm sure fans reading this will think of other scintillating performances. Towards the end of the season there was more of a feeling that Wrexham didn't want to risk losing their position in the top two slogging it out with Notts County.

The home game against Wealdstone brought three points in a 3–1 result. Next up at the Racecourse was a Woking side who looked as if they might make the play-offs. The match ended all square at 2–2, and remarkably that turned out to be the only point dropped at home in the league all season. Sixty-eight points out of a possible 69 is not a bad haul!

FAMOUS FANS FEEL THE HEAT

Those of us who have watched matches involving Wrexham for decades are very used to the fact that whichever game you watch it is never straightforward.

In February 2023 at the Recreation Ground, in the first half of their away match against Aldershot, Wrexham were in a comfortable 1–3 lead. Then just before half-time the home side halved the lead by scoring their second goal. In the second half Wrexham were often under the cosh, but with the final whistle in sight it looked as though they would hold on for a victory at a ground where they had struggled in the past. Then in the final minutes of the game Aldershot equalised. The earlier euphoria of the travelling fans turned into an all-too-familiar brand of Wrexham despair. We had thrown away two points. Then in the sixth minute of added-on time, Wrexham won a corner. Just to make fans' nerves jangle even more, one of the Aldershot players was down injured in the home team's penalty box. Finally, the corner was taken and Wrexham's Dalby, who had only been on the pitch for a couple of minutes, rose higher then anyone else and scored the winner.

Our famous co-owners were shattered after the experience of watching that game, especially the end. Sharing a photo on MatchScore, Ryan said that he may 'very well die of a cardiac event this season. Football is magic / Hell.'

Ryan Reynolds's take on that encounter at the Recreation Ground was the way the game unfolded meant that he was 'really testing the limits of appropriate drinking hours. Dear God!'

OTHER CELEBRITIES FEEL THE HEAT

As well as Rob and Ryan promoting the club in such a positive light, it's also interesting to see that many other famous people have shown interest in its amazing story. For the FA Trophy final at Wembley against Bromley, David Beckham was one of the guests of honour, along with the famous actor Will Ferrell. In February 2023 Ferrell fulfilled his promise of turning up in Wrexham to watch the match against Wealdstone, which Wrexham won 3–1. Before kick-off he delighted the manager of the Turf pub, Wayne Jones, and punters in there. In a video posted on Wrexham's Twitter feed, it has to be admitted that Will was not up to his usual acting high standards. His face was much too close to the camera and you could only see his eyes. When it came to what he said, it seemed as if he was slightly confused. Having terrible trouble with finding the right angles, he says: 'Hi, this is Will Ferrell. Where are we again?... Wrexham. I'm really excited to see the match and... I'm a little nervous.' Confused, nervous, at the wrong angle. Perhaps inebriated by the effects of the Turf pub, Will? Only a little, of course!

After that remarkable game at the Recreation Ground in Aldershot, Wrexham followed it up with a 2–0 win over Scunthorpe who at that stage of the season looked doomed for the drop. Paul Mullin, the Wrexham goal machine, got both goals.

Wrexham finished off the month of February with a 3–1 win over Dorking at home. I have to admit that Dorking were enjoyable to watch. They played an attacking open game, unlike many of the other visiting teams. I was also impressed by the Dorking fans. A good couple of hundred made the long trip to north Wales and they sang their hearts out from the first to the final whistle. It also should be mentioned that at times Wrexham fans sang along with the visiting fans. There was a great atmosphere among the bumper crowd of 10,053.

The following Tuesday, Wrexham were at the Racecourse facing Chesterfield. The visitors, who at one time had been one of the strong favourites along with Wrexham or Notts County to win the league, had been on a very poor run.

Despite this, Wrexham knew that any team managed by Paul Cook needed to be approached with huge respect. In the first half Wrexham's caution disappeared and at half-time they were up 2–0. Chesterfield looked poor in those first 45 minutes, but once they scored in the second half they had a new energy and purpose about their play and gave Wrexham a real fight. There were many among the crowd of 9,854 who were getting jittery and calling for the final whistle a long time before it went. Chesterfield's second-half performance was probably the spark they needed to rescue their season and halt the slide towards a place outside the play-offs. It certainly proved to be the case, as at the season's end they won their play-off semi-final and booked a Wembley place against Notts County.

APRIL

After the 5–1 thrashing of Oldham at the Racecourse on April Fool's Day, Wrexham prepared for a Good Friday game at the Shay against Halifax Town. There were very few Wrexham fans who had any fears about this game. After all, we'd beaten them 3–1 at home earlier in the season, while in the previous season we'd been 1–2 victors at the Shay. In addition Halifax were, by their standards, in a poor run of form. Most of the season they had been too close to the bottom of the league for their own comfort. Although Wrexham were 0–1 up at half-time, a few alarm bells started sounding: Wrexham's below-par performance, and the fact that in the second half the home team equalised, then edged ahead before securing the three points with a third goal. So Wrexham went home pointless. It also meant that Wrexham's amazing run of 29 games without defeat was at an end.

As you can imagine the Shay disappointment was a catalyst for worry in the Wrexham fan camp. We were now in the home straight of this marathon season. There were just five games to go. But if we couldn't beat Halifax, what chance did we have in the three tricky games against Barnet away, Notts County and Boreham Wood at home? What a dreadful time to hit a bad run, some of the local sages were saying.

NOTTS COUNTY

The only positive was that Notts County were due in Wrexham on Easter Monday. So we had the opportunity to put things right and move ahead on points from Notts County within three days of the Halifax setback. One of the things Rob and Ryan had often said was that you had absolutely no power or control over what was going to happen in the 90 minutes. That is just how I felt, along with the other 9,923 fans inside the ground.

The first half was end-to-end, with two very good sides going for the win. Rodriguez won a free kick for Notts County. Taken by Bostock, it was an absolute worldie of a kick which screamed its way into the top left-hand corner of the net. Foster, our goalkeeper, got close but had no chance of keeping it out. So there we were, Wrexham fans in the stadium and in various parts of the world fearing that this game could become another Halifax moment.

At the start of the second half Wrexham came out fighting. James Jones, who for me had been one of the unsung heroes of Wrexham's campaign, broke down the wing and gave a great pass for Mullin to score and make it 1–1. Cue pandemonium in the Wrexham stadium, Wrexham pubs, and all households belonging to those who followed Wrexham.

After that equalising goal, Wrexham started putting a lot of pressure on the Notts County defence. Tom O'Connor came within inches of putting Wrexham ahead, but his fabulous strike hit the bar and the ball was cleared by their defence.

At last all our pressure paid off, and Palmer played Mendy

in, who scored. Cue more pandemonium in the Wrexham stadium, Wrexham pubs... We were now 2–1 up and going for another goal to make the game safe. By the same token, Notts County were only one goal behind and they still had time to get back into the game. Palmer (not Ollie) passed to Cameron and suddenly Notts County were level at 2–2. Both sides were now going at each other hammer and tongs. It was a pulsating match, hugely enjoyable if you were a neutral, but I doubt if there were any of those in the ground. Then Elliot Lee, who had been tremendous for Wrexham all season, scored one of his signature goals with just 12 minutes remaining, 3–2 to Wrexham. At times during the season the Wrexham defence had been fantastic, but on other occasions they were slightly dire. If ever we needed them to be at their extra special best, it was now. There were 12 minutes plus of added time. All football fans know that an awful lot can happen in 12 minutes. We didn't care what happened, as long as there were no more goals. See it out, Wrexham. Please, see it out. The watch said 90 minutes were up. Still 3–2 to Wrexham. Then the referee said six more minutes. Wrexham saw them out, not comfortably, but at least were still ahead, 3–2. Then, in the seventh minute of extra time the referee awarded a penalty to Notts County. Scott stepped up to take it. (I checked that my heart spray was in my pocket. I had to watch and face the music, whether I ended up dancing for joy or prancing up and down in sheer despair.) It was a very well-struck penalty and headed for the bottom right of Foster's net. So that was it then. It was going to be 3–3. But then, as if from nowhere, Foster dived brilliantly to his right and palmed the ball away to safety. End of game. Foster had been brought in from retirement for the last seven games and in this, his third game between the sticks, he performed a miracle and ensured that Wrexham won this colossal match, 3–2.

Foster was mobbed by his fellow players and, as later YouTube footage shows, an ecstatic Ryan Reynolds caught up with him inside the changing room areas and said, 'You son of a bitch. Hell. What's that all about? You're too old for this kind of thing!' I and all Wrexham were pleased that he was not too old.

BARNET AND OTHERS

After the euphoria of beating our only serious rivals for top spot, the following Saturday we were at the Hive in Edgeware, the home of Barnet FC. Desperate to build on the glorious victory of the previous Monday, we were determined not to get stung by the Bees.

It didn't take long to realise that this match was going to drag us away from ecstasy and into the depths of tension and uncertainty. Barnet were having a good season and were anxious to consolidate a place in the play-offs. Wrexham's first-half performance was not one of their best and at half-time we were hanging on in there with a goalless draw.

Not long into the second half disaster struck when McFadzean was sent off. The rest of the game saw a dogged display from Wrexham to hold on for the point.

Three nights later we were back at the Racecourse playing Yeovil. They were fighting madly to try and avoid relegation. They put up a good fight in the first half, as they got to the interval 0–0. In the second half Wrexham improved greatly and ran out 3–0 winners. The result meant that Yeovil would definitely be playing their football in the National League South next season.

BOREHAM WOOD

Next up were Boreham Wood on Sunday, 22 April. All the other matches in the Vanarama National League had been played, so by the 6.30pm kick-off for a live televised match on BT Sport, Wrexham knew that getting three points would crown them champions. This was the third of three difficult games in the run-in to the end of the season. We have already seen that Notts County and Barnet posed problems, so there was no reason to think that this game against Boreham Wood would be any different. They possessed the best defensive record in the league and their goalkeeper was voted the best goalkeeper by the *Non-League Football Paper* and also by Adam Virgo, the BT Sports football pundit.

It's always important for a team to play themselves into a game. When the first goal went in, Wrexham certainly hadn't managed to do that. With only 45 seconds on the clock, the home team were 0–1 down. It seemed as though Ben Tozer would clear a long ball from Boreham Wood but he slipped, allowing 'Wood's striker, Lee Ndlovu, in on goal. Ben Foster rushed out to try and clear the ball, but the striker got there first and with a sumptuous lob put Boreham Wood in front.

Ryan Barnett was bought late in the season, and with his blistering pace he caused all kinds of problems for the defenders who were given the job of marking him. Barnett, with defenders flailing, got to the touchline and crossed perfectly for Elliot Lee to head home. After seven minutes of the second half, Wrexham went 2–1 in front. Mullin beat his marker, and cutting in from the left wing scored a fabulous goal, curling the ball over keeper Ashmore into the top corner.

After 70 minutes, although we were in front, it was still a bit nervy. Then Mullin ran at the defence, got past a defender, then smashed the ball past Ashmore. With ten minutes left, Wrexham were up 3–1 and this time there were no last-minute panics.

When the final whistle went there were amazing scenes as the fans invaded the pitch. Perhaps the club will be fined, but one can understand the joy of fans who had waited 15 years to get back to where Wrexham belonged in the English Football League. So Wrexham were champions and Notts

County were destined for the agonising unpredictability of the play-offs.

All the Wrexham fans I've talked with said they hoped that Notts County would join Wrexham in League Two next season. Ryan and Rob have expressed the same hope on many occasions, and I share the same view.

Despite the rain pouring down, the party started on the streets of Wrexham and lasted until 3am the following morning. One Wrexham fan put up a spoof sign on his Facebook page. It read: 'Welcome to Wrexham. Please drive slowly as the town has a hangover.' It is said that Wrexham players partied until Thursday. Who knows? More importantly, who cares?

All I know is that an awful lot of alcohol was consumed in the city after promotion was sealed. On the day of the big match against Boreham Wood, the regulars at the Turf pub drank the pub dry, and the landlord had to close the pub just before the 6.30pm kick-off. That was particularly bad news for those still queuing up to get in when the pumps ran dry!

FIXTURES AND RESULTS 2022-23

(Wrexham goal scorers in brackets)

AUGUST

6   Wrexham 2–1 Eastleigh (Lee, 2), 9,897
13   Yeovil 1–1 Wrexham (Mullin), 2,885
16   Chesterfield 2–0 Wrexham, 8,057
20   Wrexham 5–0 Maidstone (Mullin 3, 1og, Davies), 9,863
27   Woking 2–3 Wrexham (Hayden 2, Palmer), 3,185
30   Wrexham 3–1 Gateshead (Tozer, Palmer, Mullin), 9,805

SEPTEMBER

3   Dorking 0–5 Wrexham (Palmer 2, Lee, Mendy, 1og), 2,730
13   Wrexham 4–1 Dagenham (Palmer 2, Mullin 2), 9,835

17 Southend 0–0 Wrexham, 6,266

24 Wrexham 6–0 Torquay (Davies P, Mullin, Palmer, Hayden, Dalby, Forde), 9,970

OCTOBER

1   Oldham 1–2 Wrexham (Tozer, Mullin), 9,496

4   Notts County 1–0 Wrexham, 10,741

8   Wrexham 7–5 Barnet (Hayden 2, O'Connor, Palmer, Mullin 2 (1 pen), Young), 9,987

15 Blyth Spartans 1–1 Wrexham (FA Cup, 4Q) (O'Connor), 2,787

18 Wrexham 3–2 Blyth Spartans (FA Cup, 4Q replay) (Mullin, Palmer, Davies), 6,845

22 Boreham Wood 1–1 Wrexham (Hayden), 2,536

25 Wrexham 3–1 Halifax Town (Tozer, Davies, Hayden), 10,039

29 Wrexham 4–0 Altrincham (Mullin, Palmer 2, Jones), 10,107

NOVEMBER

1   Wrexham 1–0 Maidenhead (Hayden), 9,914

6   Wrexham 3–0 Oldham Athletic (FA Cup R1) (Dalby, Mullin 2), 9,113

9   Scunthorpe 1–3 Wrexham (Palmer, Hayden, Mullin), 3,569

12 Wealdstone 0–0 Wrexham, 2,817

19 Wrexham 2–0 Aldershot (Mullin, Jones), 10,071

26 Wrexham 4–1 Farnborough (FA Cup R2) (Mullin 3, Lee), 9,118

DECEMBER

3   York City 1–1 Wrexham (O'Connor), 7,145

10 Eastleigh 0–2 Wrexham (Tozer, Lee), 3,986

21 Wrexham 3–1 Scunthorpe (FA Trophy R3) (Bickerstaff, Hall-Johnson, Lee), 5,080

26 Wrexham 5–0 Solihull Moors (Palmer, Mullin 3, Hayden), 10,150

JANUARY

2   Solihull Moors 1–2 Wrexham (Tunnicliffe, O'Connor), 3,915

7   Coventry 3–4 Wrexham (FA Cup R3) (Dalby, Lee, O'Connor, Mullin), 18,218

10 Wrexham 2–1 Bromley (Mullin (pen), Jones), 9,807

13 Altrincham 2–2 Wrexham (FA Trophy R4) (Bickerstaff 2, lost on penalties), 2,526

21 Maidstone 2–3 Wrexham (Young, Mullin, Hayden), 3,341

24 Gateshead 0–3 Wrexham (O'Connor, Palmer, Mullin), 1,422

29 Wrexham 3–2 Sheffield Utd (FA Cup R4) (Jones, O'Connor, Mullin), 9,909

FEBRUARY

4   Altrincham 1–2 Wrexham (Palmer, O'Connell), 4,865

7   Sheffield Utd 3–1 Wrexham (FA Cup R4 replay) (Mullin (pen)), 20,310

11 Wrexham 3–1 Wealdstone (Mullin, Mendy, Dalby), 10,091

14 Wrexham 2–2 Woking (Forde, Mullin), 10,030

18 Aldershot 3–4 Wrexham (Mullin 2 (1pen), 1og, Dalby), 4,568

21 Wrexham 2–0 Scunthorpe (Mullin (2 pens)), 9,915

25 Wrexham 3–1 Dorking (Lee, Mullin, Dalby), 10,053

28 Wrexham 2–1 Chesterfield (Lee, Dalby), 9,854

MARCH

4   Maidenhead 2–2 Wrexham (Mullin 2), 3,534

7   Dagenham 0–4 Wrexham (Palmer 2, Mendy, Tunnicliffe), 2,772

11 Wrexham 1–0 Southend United (1og), 9,770

18 Bromley 1–2 Wrexham (Mullin 2), 5,027

25 Wrexham 3–0 York City (Dalby, Lee 1og), 10,161

APRIL

1   Wrexham 5–1 Oldham Athletic (O'Connell, Mullin 3, Lee), 9,910

7   Halifax Town 3–1 Wrexham (Lee), 7,863

10 Wrexham 3–2 Notts County (Mullin, Mendy, Lee), 9,924
15 Barnet 0–0 Wrexham, 5,265
18 Wrexham 3–0 Yeovil (Forde, Jones, Mullin), 10,106
22 Wrexham 3–1 Boreham Wood (Lee, Mullin 2), 10,126
29 Torquay 1–1 Wrexham (Lee), 4,908

TUESDAY, 2 MAY 2023 - A CITY CELEBRATES

This was the day that the triumphant team did a bus tour of the city and enjoyed the crowd's adulation. One open-deck bus carried the players, another carried the women's team, who like the men's team had won promotion, and another one carried the reserve team. The parade was due to start at 6.15pm. I made my way to the bottom of Madeira Hill and took my place outside the Nags Head. My vantage point meant that I could see the vast crowds that had already assembled at the top of Yorke Street. A buzz of excited happiness was in the air. It was good to be alive, and especially good to be a Wrexham fan. Sellers of klaxons were doing a roaring trade, as were the sellers of Wrexham scarves. Estimates of the numbers that turned out on the city's streets were as high as 40,000.

What I thought would be a half-hour wait developed into two and a half hours. I stood next to my friend Chris Bansby. My first meeting with Chris was not the best of encounters. Some seasons ago, when Kevin Wilkin was Wrexham manager, I was in the Macron Stand at half-time standing up to stretch my legs. With the noise of the music and the crowd, I didn't realise that somebody was wanting to get past me. I discovered afterwards that he had said 'Excuse me' but I obviously hadn't heard. But I did feel his stick on my leg. There's only one course of action to take when that happens, let the man with the stick through. A few weeks later I was watching Wrexham play North Ferriby in the FA Trophy final at Wembley on a big screen at my cousin's local pub. At half-time the TV cameras panned the crowd. Suddenly, there was a profile of the man with the stick. I pointed and said, 'I'm sure I know that guy.' My cousin looked at the man on the screen, then said, 'You should, he's your neighbour. He lives on the opposite side of the street, about four doors down.'

After that I got to know him and we became good friends. So, waiting for the bus to turn up with the players, it was great to stand next to someone I knew and someone who knows his football inside out. As we talked he sang the praises of Phil Parkinson, despite the fact that one of his friends, who had watched Parkinson manage Sunderland in the past, claimed that he was very defensive. That's not an accusation I would lay at his door. As far as I'm concerned he strikes me as tactically bright. He has certainly created a Wrexham side which likes to attack and is great to watch when they are moving forward. Chris also felt that one difference between Phil Parkinson and previous managers was that he had obviously spent a lot of time working with the players on what to do off the ball.

Inevitably, waiting for this Vanarama National League championship winning side to appear gave us time to have a long chat about where this team could go. Chris felt they would probably make it into the Championship, but wondered whether there was the infrastructure to sustain a Premiership team. There would certainly be a need to rebuild the Racecourse if that were possible, or even relocate to a new stadium.

During the wait Chris used his mobile phone to follow the progress of the bus. He became the most popular person in our section of the crowd. At one stage a woman peered at the screen and said, 'They're outside my house. If I'd known, I'd have stayed in the garden.'

There were others who clearly didn't know anything about the bus tour. A bemused-looking woman with a dog stood for a long time staring at us. Then a young father passed us, as he pushed his infant up the hill. And then someone drove up Yorke Street, with the crowds almost pressing against the sides of his vehicle. Eventually police and stewards intervened and told him to turn around.

At eight o'clock a huge roar went up as the first of the three open-deck buses edged its way into the far end of the street. A girl behind me said to her father, 'We've waited all this time to see the players and they'll only be here for five minutes.' Her father replied, 'Yes, but those five minutes will stay with you for the rest of your life.' It's a little known fact, outside of Wrexham, that the city is crammed full of philosophers.

And at last the players were there right in front of me. It's amazing how different some of them look all dressed up, without their shorts and tops. They must have been exhausted and probably quite cold, but still they had smiles for us all. The buses had been held up by the sheer volume of fans along the route. It was great to see them. I felt I was one small part of a huge sea of people showing our gratitude for what the players had done for us and the city.

A day or so after the parade, Rob and Ryan told the players that they were being taken to Las Vegas on a four-day all-expenses-paid trip.

And so we say thanks to all those who have brought so much joy to the city, and to individuals who have followed the club throughout the years. We are now back where we all believe we should be. Back in the English Football League.

Normally the close season is very quiet and we football fans might watch cricket instead, or if that's not to our liking even go on holiday. But the 2023 close season is going to be very different. We will be scouring maps and fixture lists to see who will be coming to the Racecourse, and where travelling fans will end up going to during next season.

Some fans will be delighted that Notts County will be joining us in the higher league. Others are not so certain. They have not forgiven County for pushing us so hard in the season. The Magpies won a pulsating play-off final at Wembley, defeating Chesterfield on penalties.

In addition, many Wrexham fans will be travelling to America where Wrexham will take part in a tournament where they'll play a Chelsea and Manchester United side.

THE END.

OR JUST THE BEGINNING?

Also from Y Lolfa:

£9.99

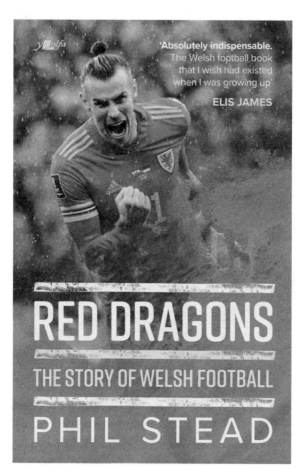

'Absolutely indispensable.
The Welsh football book
that I wish had existed
when I was growing up'

ELIS JAMES

RED DRAGONS

THE STORY OF WELSH FOOTBALL

PHIL STEAD

£14.99

Dixie

The Autobiography of Dixie McNeil

£9.95